Carry On Travelling

– J.D. RAYNER –

An environmentally friendly book printed and bound in England by
www.printondemand-worldwide.com

This book is made entirely of chain-of-custody materials

www.fast-print.net/store.php

CARRY ON TRAVELLING

Names have been changed to protect the innocent

A catalogue record for this book is available from the British Library

ISBN 978-178035-798-0

First published 2014 by
FASTPRINT PUBLISHING
Peterborough, England.

Authors note

Since writing *Travelling with Grumpy* some names have changed but the people remain the same. Petal, my wife of over 30 years is now Nettie, the matriarch of the family. She is the glue that keeps us all together. Princess is still the matriarch-in-waiting and joined to the hip with our son Junior. He is becoming increasingly eccentric and xenophobic. I don't know where he gets it from, the xenophobia that is. Cinders has set new standards for cleaning. She can now get concrete to shine! The grandchildren continue to delight, more about them in 'Nice One Monaco Too'. Ash is someone who I've spent an increasing amount of time with lately and calls me by my initial 'Jay' as does Lady F who tracked me down for a family history trip to Poland.

Contents

Burgundy

22-09-12

The late summer sun shines brightly in the sky. Autumn will have to wait a little longer to impose itself. The family are enjoying an all too rare get together and as these occasions are becoming less frequent, when they do happen, they are all the more enjoyable because of it. We are in good spirits, swapping stories about where we have been, either together or separately when Ash turns up unexpectedly. I haven't seen him for ages so it is a real treat. Ash knows where to find us. He is a big man with an indecently large mop of curly hair and a waistline that bears testament to many fine lunches. He is by trade a wandering minstrel, which is why his visits are infrequent and random. He has a slack G-string that I keep reminding him about whenever we meet.

'Have you fixed it yet?' I ask.

'The G-string? No, I'm comfortable with it as it is thank you.'

'I thought you are supposed to be as one with your instrument, finely tuned and all that.'

'For classical music that maybe so, but with my particular genre, an understanding will do. As you know, I do not caress my instruments, I tame them and then I train them. It takes a while but in the end they know who the boss is and sound sweet enough when I play them.'

Ash then sits down, pours himself a very large glass of wine before telling us the purpose of his visit. He looks directly at me and says, 'I'm planning a trip to France to do some shopping and I need a navigator. Do you fancy a trip?'

He has barely finished the sentence when the laughter rings out long and loud, so much so that it brings complaints from the neighbours four doors away! Ash is not impressed.

Junior then chips in with his own observations. 'Why take him? He struggles to get out of the road on his own, he uses a sat-nav to find the town centre and if he goes beyond that he takes an overnight bag with him.'

More laughter.

'How do you put up with all this?' he asks me.

'Selective hearing,' I reply.

Ash is getting cross. He is a man of few words and hates being interrupted. Finally he manages to get a word in and is straight to the point.

'I need him because he can speak enough French to do some translating for me. Can any of you others speak the language as well as he does?'

Silence.

'I thought not, so that is why I need him. As for navigating, I will work out the route and he can read the signs for me to make sure that I don't stray too far off track.'

He then pours himself another very large glass of wine, which he gulps down in an indecently short space of time before departing.

'I'll be in touch,' he says and disappears.

He is as good as his word and phones me a few days later.

'I've fixed up the trip. You'll need an overnight bag and I'll pick you up at 06-30 on Thursday the fifth. Will that be okay?'

'Certainly will Ash. I'll be ready.'

That is how abrupt and straight to the point Ash is. It doesn't suit everyone but it suits me because one knows exactly where one stands with him. Besides, I fancy a few days away even if it is at short notice. Over the course of the next few days I wait for the right moment to inform Nettie of my latest escapade. Her reply is as I expect.

'If you're going shopping is there any chance that you can bring me a few things back?' she asks.

'If we go to a hypermarket then possibly I can, if we have the time.'

'If you aren't going to a hypermarket where are you going to do your shopping?'

'At a vineyard my dear; Ash is going to try and find a certain vineyard that he found accidentally when minstrelling last year.'

'Is that a proper word?'

'What, minstrelling?'

'Yes.'

'I don't know but I use it to describe the activity of one, in this case Ash, who is a minstrel.'

'When are you going?' Nettie asks me, having decided that sensible answers are in short supply.

'Thursday morning and I am being picked up at 06-30. I'll be away for two nights. Is that okay?'

'Can't you make it three?' she asks sarcastically.

05-10-12

The day arrives. Ash turns up on time and we are off. The drive to Dover is a joy as the traffic flows freely. We see the autumnal colours on the trees. The pale greens turning yellow and orange but not yet brown. The sea looks flat calm as we catch our first glimpse of it from the motorway.

Once through formalities we eat an instantly forgettable breakfast and Ash decides to go for a walk on deck. I try to read a book but cannot settle, which is unusual for me. Our immediate destination is Dunkirk, which for some reason, Ash prefers over Calais.

After disembarking we head to the nearest filling station to top up the tank with diesel. As we pull away

Ash turns to me and says in a puzzled way, 'You're a bit quiet Jay, what's the matter?'

'Nothing's the matter. It's just that every time I come to Dunkirk I think of Dad. I used to bring him here on day trips, which he enjoyed, and then one day he said to me that he'd jumped in a canal around here and wondered if we could find the spot.'

'When was this?' he asks.

'Must have been late 1999 because after that I had to do a recce with him to sort out a restaurant for when he and his Dunkirk Veteran mates had finished their 60th anniversary parade.'

'So what's the story?'

'The first part was to find the place where he jumped into the canal on his way back to the Dunkirk beaches. I looked at the map and suggested the D916 road to Bergues. He said it was the right road because it had a railway line on one side of it and a canal on the other. So I sorted out a day trip for him and we came over specifically for that reason. He said that if we get to the town we'd have driven too far. I suggested that if he sees the spot then he should tell me but in any case I'd drive to Bergues, we'd have a coffee stop and then look again on the way back because that would have been the direction he'd have been travelling in back in 1940. He thought that was a good idea.

On the way back, after our coffee break, we came to the spot where he thought it was and as luck would have it there was a gap in the hedge where I could park the car. He looked around and decided that it was the spot although the trees on the other side of the canal were bigger than he remembered. I pointed out that trees tend to grow a bit in sixty years! Satisfied that it was the place I took a photo of him at the spot but to this day I've no idea where it is. It's probably in a safe place knowing me.

That was that and I gave it no more thought until he phoned me up and explained that he was going on the 60th anniversary parade and would like to fix up a meal afterwards in Merville for a coach load of old soldiers. I asked him what his problem was and he said that he'd like to go to the restaurant in person and book it. Could I fix it up for him? I said I'd look in to it and he said well don't be too long because he had a committee meeting in a couple of months and he wanted to have something sorted out.

Anyway, I sorted out an itinerary and told him that it would be a long day. There wouldn't be much slack time so punctuality was essential and he could have one hour in the café and one hour shopping on the way back if he wanted. He seemed okay with the arrangements, ran it past the committee and the next thing I know is I have to take him and two other committee members.'

'What if you'd refused?' asks Ash.

'I couldn't see it being an option, not after I'd given my word. You know me, once I say I'll do something, I'll do it.'

'Fair point; so how did the day go?'

'Very well as it happens; punctuality was never going to be a problem because the old soldiers were used to the discipline. What did spook me a bit was when we travelled through the Fôret de Nieppe. The old boys were chatting away quite happily then as we entered the woods they stopped and it was eerily silent until one of them in the back asked the other one in the back if this was the place. He replied that it was and that he was in here for twenty days. Two-dozen of them had entered but only three came out. There was more silence and then the first speaker said to me that we were nearly out of the woods and the town was not far away. Can you imagine that; driving through someone's memories?'

'It's something I've never done and I'm not in any hurry to do it either. What happened then?'

'When I'd driven out of the forest the chatting started up again as though nothing had happened. I parked the car outside the restaurant which we found more by luck than judgement. Dad's memory was not the sharpest when it comes to navigating and sadly I think I have inherited it as I am constantly being reminded. I told them that I'd have a sleep in the car while they did the negotiating. They were having none of it and said that I was expected to translate because Dad had said I could speak French.'

'No pressure then!'

'As it happened I wasn't needed because the crafty old proprietor plied them with drink during the negotiating. After three or four drinks they could all speak the native tongue fluently. I told them what they had arranged and they said that I'd got it all wrong. Outnumbered as I was I didn't argue but knew that I was right and they were wrong. It wasn't a big deal but Dad did think that I had probably got it wrong citing driving fatigue as the reason. The drive back was quiet as they all fell asleep. It was just as well I didn't join them or we'd all have been in trouble! When we arrived at the Channel Tunnel they sprang into life ready to do some shopping.'

'Typical. The drive back is always the worst because the excitement of the day has gone and that's what happens. Don't you fall asleep on me Jay!'

'Not a chance.'

'What happened on the day?'

'What day?'

'The 60th anniversary of Dunkirk.'

'The parade started in the town square and the old boys were made to stand for an hour until all the dignitaries had arrived, Prince Charles among them. He inspected the troops, then there were the speeches and finally the parade marched off. Interestingly enough, of all the dignitaries, only Prince Charles spoke in both English and French. What the television coverage did not capture was the level of noise from the crowd. When the band started up the old soldiers stood a little taller and when they heard the noise from the crowd they were twenty-year old men in eighty-year old bodies. For one moment I half expected some of the wheelchair contingent to have a "Lazarus" moment and jump out of their wheelchairs. The noise from the crowd was deafening. It was "Beatlemania" all over again. Old ladies in the crowd were pressing forward to try and touch the soldiers. They expressed their undying love for them. "We will never forget you Tommy." "Sank you zo much Tommy." "We love you all". It was an emotional march. Prince Charles took the salute and he looked totally bewildered by it all. He has seen many things in his time but I'm sure that took him completely by surprise.

The march was for one kilometre and at the end of it one old soldier collapsed and died. Dad said that was better than at the 50th anniversary when eleven died. Maybe some of them shouldn't have marched but who is going to be brave enough to tell them that they cannot march in memory of their old comrades. I wouldn't be that person. I couldn't be that person.

Back at the hotel the old boys had gone from being twenty-year olds to looking 120 years old. It had taken its toll but they had all done what they'd set out to do. In the morning they were all suited and booted and ready to do it all over again at De Panne in Belgium. It was a smaller affair but just as sincere. Pushing a wheelchair over cobbled stones was a bit of a challenge but I managed it. Dad had had a great weekend and as it was the last ever official parade for the Dunkirk Veterans I suppose I took part, in a small way, in a bit of history. Certainly as time passes by I think back to it and feel privileged to have been there. So to answer your question about why I am quiet in Dunkirk, it is because every time I come here it all comes back to me, that's why. Now where exactly are we off to?'

'The Burgundy region, to buy some wine from a certain vineyard that I know of.'

By now we are getting on to the toll roads and so I reach out of the window, pick up the ticket from the toll booth and settle into my seat as Ash drives along the motorway. The crops fascinate me as the same ones are riper and more advanced in growth the further south we get. Near the coast the maize is still green and is similar to how it is in England whereas now, half way down France it is brown and looks ready to harvest.

After driving for most of the day we pull in to our overnight stop just outside Auxerre on an industrial estate. It is just off the motorway and in the early days could have been a staging post on the long road south. There are several hotels, restaurants and a lorry park. It is not the sort of place for a prolonged stay but is ideal for an overnight stop. After freshening up we go to the hotel next door for a meal, Ash cannot string a sentence together in French because he only speaks 'Restaurant French', so I rely on him to tell me what some of the items are on the menu as they go way beyond the 'A' level syllabus. Between us we get along just fine. Two bottles of superb red wine later and we are putting the world to rights. If we imbibe a third, which we don't, there wouldn't be any need for the U.N. because we will have solved all the world's problems!

While we are rambling on, we discuss Peru and it is one of the few places that I have been to that Ash hasn't.

'If you get the chance to go take it,' I tell him. 'Cuzco, the old Inca capital, is one of my all time favourite cities. It is 10,000 feet above sea level and as the air is thinner at that altitude everything is done at a much slower pace and that suits me fine. Just off the main square there is a café run by a European man with his hair tied back in a ponytail. He looked for all the world like he was an ageing hippy who had arrived in Cuzco one day, put down his back pack and decided that he had had enough of wandering and that it was time to put down some roots. The café was spotless. His ice cubes that he proudly advertised were made from bottled water. Do you know what the national dish of Peru is?'

'No.'

'It's guinea pig. It is a fast breeding animal, cheap to keep and provides a bit of meat for the domestic table. In restaurants it is the sauce that gives it some flavour. In truth there isn't too much meat on a guinea pig and without the sauce it tastes a bit like rabbit.'

'I'll bear that in mind,' says Ash who is now showing signs of fatigue after a long day of driving.

06-10-12

It is a new day and a new start for us. We enjoy a superb continental breakfast enhanced by the best baguettes I've eaten in France, check out of the hotel and head for Irancy, which is just a short drive away.

'I hope you are ready for this Jay,' says Ash.

'Ready for what?' I reply.

'Wine tasting.'

'At 09-00 in the morning!'

'Yes.'

'I don't normally drink before midday.'

'Well you will today. Not so much drink it as taste it, pontificate, mumble a few words, spit or swallow, it's up to you and then mark it accordingly. I will have to spit as I'm driving but you can choose what to do.'

'It all sounds very simple. How many do we get to taste?'

'That depends on how knowledgeable we appear to be.'

'Okay, I'll do my best Ash. It'll be something to put on my CV of life, drinking after breakfast.'

'Not drinking; tasting. There is a difference.' he reminds me.

We find the tasting area tucked away in the valley between the fields of vines. Ash recognises the ruddy-faced man, as the son of the owner, who greets us as we drive into the small car park. He speaks no English so it is up to me to translate. As Ash is driving he just sips and spits but when the seller realises that I am not driving he fills my glass just a little more generously. It loosens the vocabulary restraints and improves the accent no end. The wine seller tells us that some of the vines have been replaced by cherry orchards. He then points out the fields where the grapes are grown that apply to each of the wines that we have tasted. We are then given a tour of the vats that the new wine is in.

'What is the quality like?' I ask.

'The quality will be good for 2012 but the quantity will be down due to the unfavourable weather conditions.'

We make our purchases and as much as I would like to pull a cork when I get home I am told that I must leave the wine for two more years for it to mature, in order for it to reach optimum taste. I don't know how patient I shall be but I do know that there is a strong tannin taste to it at the moment.

With the main purpose of our mini trip complete we drive around some delightfully narrow roads where the cars are few and far between. The scenery is stunning. We stop by a river in the village of Rochers du Saussoir for a leg stretch and to take a few pictures. There is a row of old houses built at the foot of some bulbous rocks, and on the rocks are a team of rock climbers. Rather them than me, I think to myself. In the twenty minutes that we stop here we only see one car go past. Weeping willows hang over the river and almost touch the surface of the water that ripples in the faintest of breezes.

All too soon we are on the move again as Ash continues to take me on a trip down his memory lane. Our destination this time is Vezelay. The car is parked and like me, Ash is drawn to churches, not from a religious point of view but from an architectural point of view, so that is where we head. This particular one is medieval and is one of the finest examples of its type and has been used in many films, so he informs me. The houses next to it are built in a style that could have come straight out of a fairy story. There is a small area to the side of the church that has been given over to archaeologists who have discovered evidence of buildings from bygone ages where one era has built upon a building from a different era. That posed a question for the archaeologists as to how much should they remove and how much they should keep. In the end they kept bits of each era so that one can see how the site developed over the centuries.

Our site seeing is brief, we move on to Auxerre and check into our hotel. This is altogether a better establishment with its own secure parking lot and just five minutes walk from the main square. As we make our way towards the river I recognise the place straight away. I have been here with Ash on a boating holiday thirty years ago. This is my first visit back here since then but it is the tenth for him. It is the smell of the fermented grape that keeps tempting him back!

'I remember this place,' I say to Ash as we are standing on a bridge over the river.

'Do you see that baker's shop over there?' he says as he points it out.

'Yes.'

'That's where I used to get the bread from when we were on that boating holiday all those years ago.'

'How do you remember stuff like that?'

'I've been back regularly since then so I remember random stuff.'

'You certainly do,' I say. 'I suppose you can even point out the restaurant that we ate our one and only meal in when we splashed the cash instead of cooking for ourselves on the boat.'

'Of course, and just a bit more useless information for you, it has changed hands since then.'

'From that holiday onwards Ash, I started to follow the fortunes of the Auxerre football team in the newspapers and how well they did largely thanks to one man, Guy Roux who was with them for 44 years until he retired in 2009.'

'And as you know Jay, I'm not interested in football but I was here when Liverpool were back in Europe for the first time since their European ban following the Heysel disaster. Needless to say there was a heavy police presence and not being a football fan I decided to leave before the fans turned up.'

We move on and go inside the huge cathedral of Saint-Etienne. We pay to visit the treasury and the crypt, which is a thousand years old. It is in remarkably good condition even though some of the plaster has come off the frescos. The colours on what remains are still vibrant. In the treasury, there are papers and other church artefacts that are in equally good condition. Some of the documents go back to an age before printing and the handwriting is astonishingly good.

After the visit to the cathedral we make our way back to the footbridge over the River Yonne and just stay on the top of it to gaze at the scenery. It has always been a rich area and the old buildings bear testament to it. Boating holidays now make up a good part of the waterway traffic whereas in days gone by the river had been a lifeline to all forms of commercial traffic. As the sun is beginning to lose its heat we decide that we have done our bit of culture for one day and seek out a bar for a couple of beers before finding a suitable place to eat.

07-10-12

Once again the alarm on my phone doesn't go off and then the awful truth dawns on me. My phone is still set to British time and not French time which is an hour ahead! It doesn't matter as we are up in good time and have breakfast before starting the long journey home.

'I think we'll take a different route home Jay. We'll go around the Peripherique and avoid Paris. Is that okay with you?'

'You're driving so do what's best for you.'

'That's the plan anyway,' Ash replies none too confidently.

We clear the city of Auxerre easily enough and as we head north up the motorway I notice a crop in a field that looks like bamboo, whether it is or not, I don't know. If it is I suppose there must be a market for it with furniture and fencing made from the stuff so if the French can grow it then why not do so and save on imports. Our conversation is sporadic, as it was on the way down, so I amuse myself by checking off the motorway junctions on the map that I have on my lap.

The crops are getting greener, the sky's becoming darker and the sun is hiding behind the clouds. The weather forecast has been for rain over southern England through the night and for the front to move south. That front is what we are now going under, hence the change in climate.

By now we are getting closer to Paris and the traffic is becoming noticeably heavier. The Peripherique is its usual manic self and as we follow the signs the only landmark that I recognise is the Sacre Cœur, all the rest of the buildings are ugly concrete blocks. We find our exit and then we hit a snag, the signposts stop being helpful. Ash has no idea where he is.

'Jay I think I'm lost. Have you any idea where we are?'

To say Paris would not be helpful.

'No need to panic Ash; we'll use basic navigation. I have a compass with me that I usually take when I'm out walking so we'll use that.'

'How will that help?' he asks.

'It's simple. I know we need to get to Dunkirk but that's not signposted from here but Calais is. We know that Calais is north of Paris so all we do is take any road going north. If we get to a junction then we take whichever road is nearest to the northerly direction. Sooner or later we will come to a signpost that reads Calais, because that is indicated from a long way out, or we'll see one that indicates the motorway that we are looking for. Either way we will be getting further and further from Paris.'

'Are you sure this will work?'

'Certain,' I say. 'I've done this once before when I drove along the Champs Elysees from Place de la Concorde to the Arc de Triomphe and then wanted the road to Calais. I knew that I needed to turn right but the signs were not much help so, as I hadn't got a compass, I turned to another form of basic navigation, the sun.'

'How did that help?'

'As it was the afternoon I needed to keep the sun on my left and whatever road I took I had to keep the sun on my left. Sooner or later I knew I'd find a sign to Calais. Mind you it took me through some areas of Paris that you won't find on the tourist map and no doubt this will happen today. Never fear it will work out.'

I don't think Ash is totally convinced but he is willing to give it a try. After negotiating some narrow side streets we come to a tree-lined road that we drive down. At the bottom, some 300 metres away I see a 'T' junction and I say to Ash, 'We need to turn left as we are now heading east.'

Once we reach the junction we find a signpost for the A16 motorway. Mightily relieved Ash follows the signs and we eventually make it onto the road that we are looking for. In truth I don't suppose it added any extra time to our journey and just goes to show that there are alternatives to sat-navs!

By now we have passed underneath the weather front. The sky is blue again and the sun, warm through the windscreen. As we make our way along the motorway, inland from Boulogne, we can see the white cliffs of Dover. I have seen them before across the Channel but never as clear as it is today. It is quite a magnificent sight, Boulogne in the foreground, then the English Channel and then Dover in the background, as clear as Ash's face, who is sitting next to me, We drive on past Calais to Dunkirk, make a quick visit to the hypermarket, before making our way to the terminal, check in and board the ferry.

It has been a terrific weekend and I am look forward to getting home so that I can pull a cork, not from one of the bottles purchased at the vineyard but from a bottle that I have put aside to share with Nettie when I get indoors. What I hadn't planned on was Nettie anticipating my intentions. I had remembered to buy a few things for her at the hypermarket plus a surprise present, which was well received, and then she led me to the lounge where the bottle of wine had already been opened, candles lit and nobody to disturb us.

'Now tell me Jay, how was the trip?' she purred.

I tell her the story as she looked at me in a way that indicated she wasn't listening and when I'd finished she says to me in a measured way, 'It sounds like you've had too good a time without me so I better do something about it hadn't I?'

Agadir

I didn't have to wait long for Nettie to come up with something. She's full of good ideas!

'As you know, I don't like the cold weather and winter just seems to go on for too long, so I've decided that we are off to Agadir, just the two of us. What do you think?'

'It's a song isn't it?'

'Not Agadoo, Agadir; it's in Morocco and further south than Marrakech so it should be warm.'

'Sounds good to me; when are we going?'

'Soon.'

10-11-12

Getting out of bed in the dark on a cold and chilly November morning is not my idea of fun but it is something I am prepared to do if it means we are going on one of our trips. While Nettie is getting herself together I make my way to the kitchen and heat up the leftovers from last nights Chinese takeaway, to have for my breakfast. I rarely start the day without a breakfast even if this is one of my more unusual choices.

We leave home at 05-45 and drive to Gatwick. The drive, thankfully, is without incident and we arrive in plenty of time to check in the one suitcase that she has insisted on bringing. I think about asking her why she has brought a suitcase or why she insisted on being so early when, at home, if we are invited out, it is her default setting that we are ten minutes late! I think about it but that's all I do. I know my place and usually it's in the wrong!

Eventually, after an interminably long wait, we board the plane and three and half hours later we are in Agadir, a happy lady, a suitcase and me. We find our way through formalities, board a minibus and thirty minutes after that we arrive at our hotel and check into our room. Unfortunately we are as far away from reception as it is possible to get. There are so many corridors, twists and turns between the two, that if the architect of this hotel had been in charge of tunnelling in *'The Great Escape'* they'd still be digging today and with no idea of where they were!

'Don't let me get lost dearest,' I plead with Nettie.

'You'll be fine,' she tries to reassure me.

'Keep your phone on just in case.'

'You're being over-dramatic.'

I leave it at that and hope for the best.

We unpack; have a wash and a change of clothes before heading out for an evening meal. We don't have to venture too far as there are plenty of restaurants to choose from opposite the hotel. As we are in Morocco we just have to have a tagine to get us in the mood for our stay here. I opt for a chicken with lemon and it is as much as I can do to finish it after I have eaten most of the olives and bread that are put on the table as an appetiser. Nettie chooses a fish tagine.

It is while we are enjoying the meal and feeling smug about being warmer than we would have been in England that I turn to the good lady and ask, 'Did you let Junior know where we were going?'

'No, I thought that you'd be doing it,' she replies slightly concerned.

'Not to worry, I'll send him a text. I did tell him we were going away but I didn't say where we were going exactly.'

'Make sure you tell him where we are.'

'Yes dear.'

I haven't been entirely truthful with Junior because his xenophobia is getting worse. I told him we were going away but I didn't tell him when we were going or where, because if he knew the exact date he'd play up and cause his mother to worry, when what she needs to do is to unwind and relax. I don't know where he gets his xenophobia from because neither of us suffers from it so it can't be hereditary. He is okay with us being away in England and Western Europe, provided we don't stay too long, but mention Eastern Europe or Africa and he freaks out. Any mention of the other continents and he turns ashen. I think he may even be a secret member of the Flat Earth Society!

Text to Junior: ***Arrived safely. No time difference from U.K. All is well.***

11-11-12

We are in no rush to eat breakfast, as we have to meet our holiday rep at midday, so it gives us time to 'people watch' and linger over our croissants and coffee. To while away a bit more time until the appointed hour, we stroll around the impressively maintained gardens and explore some more of the hotel's corridors, which totally disorientate me at the moment.

Midday arrives and we are seated in the reception area listening to the rep outline what trips are available. He wants us to decide there and then and part with our money but we decide to wait a while, talk it over and then decide which trips, if any, we will take, although we sign up for the city tour later on in the day. That is the last we see of him, even though he should call in every day, he doesn't. The Invisible Man would be easier to find!

The city tour proves a good way to orientate ourselves. The first stop is at the Marina, which is at one end of the 6km long promenade, to see the wealthy people's playground. From here we take a short steep climb up to the highest point to look down over the fishing port and the town. We are told that Agadir means 'wall enclosing a fortress or town' in the Berber language and is situated in the southwest of Morocco on the Atlantic coast just north of the River Souss. Earthquakes have destroyed it twice, once in 1731 and more recently in 1960. The present city was built just two kilometres south of the epicentre. Prior to 1960 it was all desert. After admiring the views, taking some pictures and running the gauntlet of camel drovers, who all insist we have a camel ride, which we decline, we make our way across to the far side of town to visit the souks. We don't go in to enjoy the delights of the place, due to a lack of time, so we just make a note of its location. From here it is but a short ride to one of the mosques, which we can admire from the outside but are not allowed to go inside. Next, we go to a factory that is selling argan oil. We are told that it is made from the kernels of the argan tree and that the tree only grows in Morocco. The oil has many benefits, which Nettie picks up on, but the only thing that grabs my attention is the fact that the prices in the factory are about ten times the price elsewhere. It is a good product as I find out later in the week when Nettie applies some to her hair. It gives it a very healthy look and that is just one of its many uses.

The last visit on this tour is a quick visit to a massage parlour where we are told that we can have a massage 'at a special price, cheaper than hotel!' There is no end to the enthusiasm that people have for getting us to part with our Dirham. We say, 'We'll think about it,' which we do, but not for long.

Back at the hotel we mull over the tour, have a better idea of our orientation and celebrate with a few vodkas before going out to dinner. We decide to head in the opposite direction from the first night and walk along the red tiled promenade. There are millions of tiles along the whole length of the seafront with a few grey ones to break the monotony. Whoever had the contract for supplying them must have been a very happy man. Meanwhile, my curiosity is getting the better of me as I search hotel rooftops for the web cam that puts the pictures on the Internet. Thankfully I find it so we don't have to spend too long rooftop gazing because the temperature has dropped and the air is nippy.

We find a suitable place to eat and, sticking with the Moroccan theme, I choose a mixed fish dish and a bottle of local red wine while Nettie has white wine with her fish dish. At this point events become hazy as the mix of the vodka from earlier and the red wine began to kick in. Somehow I arrive back at the hotel and send my daily text message.

Text to Junior: ***Did city tour. Sunshine all day. Found web cam.***

12-11-12

I wake up feeling out of sorts but with no headache. I have no recollection of getting back to the hotel last night so decide to ask Nettie. 'Good morning gorgeous, how are you this fine morning?'

'Don't you "gorgeous" me!' she replies rather abruptly.

'What have I done now?' I ask in all innocence.

'You were in a state last night. You were all over the place getting back here. It took me ages to steer you in the right direction. Do you remember anything from last night?'

'I remember feeding the fish heads from my meal to the resident cat that was prowling around the tables looking for scraps.'

'You nearly adopted the cat!'

'I remember paying the bill.'

'You've got that bit right, except somehow the money went from your wallet to the waiter via the floor. Watching you two scrabbling around on the floor trying to retrieve the money, while the breeze was blowing it further away, each time you put a hand out to grab a note, was entertainment enough for the whole restaurant to stop and stare.'

'I remember leaving the restaurant, then it goes blank and I recall sending a text message to Junior, that bit I am sure of. The only bit that I have no recall of is the walk back from the restaurant to here.'

'Let me fill you in on the blanks. The walk back took over an hour when it should have been no more than ten minutes, fifteen at the most. If I hadn't have been there, you would have fallen off the promenade several times, you would have bought goodness knows how many trinkets from the souvenir sellers that were still out late at night, waiting for vulnerable people like you and to cap it all you tried to kiss the security guard at the hotel gate. I was not impressed!'

'Sorry dearest one.'

'Don't "sorry" me. Go for a walk and clear your head.'

'Can I have breakfast first?' I plead.

'You're unbelievable!' Nettie spat the words out through gritted teeth. 'After breakfast I'm staying by the pool all day and you're going for a walk! Understood?'

'Yes dear.'

Breakfast is eaten in silence but with each passing mouthful I start to get back to my old self.

'There isn't much English being spoken is there?' says Nettie in a tone of voice that belies the tirade directed at me in the bedroom.

'Not much,' I reply. 'It sounds mostly French with a bit of German and Russian thrown in.'

'I agree. Now I'm ready for a hard day in the sun by the pool, so I suggest you go for a walk. When you get back you know where I'll be.'

So without further ado, now that we have cleared the air, I decide to go for that walk.

Our hotel is situated half way along the promenade so I decide to walk towards the marina and make a note of facilities along the way. The sad fact is that it could be anywhere along the Mediterranean coastline and not the Moroccan coastline because many of the restaurants look like that is where they belong. I note Lebanese, Indian, Thai and Gulf and Arabic plus an excellent ice cream parlour. On the beach each hotel has its own cordoned off area with sunbeds and sunshades, there is jet-ski hire and a beach patrol on quad bikes.

My slow walk has taken me to the marina where expensive craft lay tied up on moorings, displaying a wealth that the seafront hawkers can only dream of. I wander around it hoping to find a way to the fishing port but fail to do so. On retracing my steps to the hotel I feel obliged to report back to Nettie. It's just as well I do as she has fallen asleep and is beginning to burn. Upon hearing me she wakes up, grunts, turns over and adopts a new sun-worshipping position and goes back to sleep. I decide to go for another walk!

This time I venture into unchartered territory on another fact-finding mission. I go out of the front of the hotel, turn left past restaurants, a travel agents, a British pub, a bridge, more restaurants and souvenir shops until I find, set back from the road, an entrance to a zoo. It has a pathway that leads to the next street back so I walk through the zoo and look at some of the colourful species that are held in captivity. Some of the birdcages I feel are too small but the birds looked healthy enough. When I finally reach the street at the upper level I find another travel agents so I go in and seek out a price list for trips to see how they compare to the ones on offer from our non-appearing holiday rep. I consult my town map and start to build a picture of where things are, so I make my way back. This fresh air is doing me a power of good.

I am just about to start a conversation with Nettie, now that I have joined her by the swimming pool and have got myself comfortable, but the music is turned up louder. I have to shout to make myself heard, 'I've found a few more places to visit and……'

'What did you say?'

'I said that…..'

'I can't hear you. Speak up.'

'I'm going for another walk. I can't stand that racket

any more.'

I go out of the back of the hotel and head for the promenade. Instead of turning right towards the marina, I turn left to see where the red tiled promenade leads. I walk until it ends, noting that the hotels have become progressively grander. There are some hotels beyond the red tiles of the promenade so at this point I walk along the beach and am curious to see what lays beyond the ridge of sand in the distance. The amount of people on the beach has lessened. On the water's edge there are a couple walking hand in hand and going in the same direction as I am. We keep going until we are the only ones left. The tracks of the quad bike beach patrol have ended; there are no more footprints in the sand beyond them but we keep walking. A whistle sounds. I take no notice. The couple at the water's edge look at each other then carry on walking. I do the same. The whistle sounds again, more urgent than before. They look at each other, I look at them and they look at me. We carry on walking. The whistle sounds a third time, a uniformed man jumps up and down outside a small hut situated at the top of the beach, waving frantically at us, indicating that we must turn back. We do. Neither of us finds out what is beyond the ridge. I imagine unexploded bombs and that it is a safety issue, the reality, as I find out a few days later, is that it is the King's private beach. Oops!

Back at the hotel I find my beloved still by the pool, having turned a darker shade of brown. How dark is difficult to say as I haven't brought my colour chart with me but if the look of satisfaction on her face is anything to go by then it scores well. We make our way back to the bedroom and I decide to send a text to Junior. I turn on my phone, just to refresh my memory of what I'd sent last night. I read the text. ***'Fed the cat.'*** I'm mortified. I don't remember sending that so as a damage limitation exercise I decide to say nothing! Junior hasn't even replied to seek an explanation.

Text to Junior: ***Quiet day. Went walking. Too much noise by the swimming pool for me.***

13-11-12

We are woken up by a seagull tapping on the wood of our balcony. If it thinks we are a feeding opportunity for an easy breakfast it is mistaken. Nettie is in fine form and she has it in mind that we will go shopping in the main souk today. To get there we hire one of the small taxis that can only ply their trade within the city limits. They are all orange coloured. In Marrakech they are fawn and in another town sky blue. Inside the souk, which is a covered market, there is everything imaginable for sale. The fake watches and designer labels do nothing for me but the fruit and vegetables do. They are arranged in gravity defying heaps in a most artistic way. It almost seems a shame to buy anything that would spoil the shape, so we don't! The meat section has live poultry. The purchaser selects a bird and the vendor kills and plucks it there and then so it's not a place for the squeamish. On the positive side, meat doesn't get any fresher than this, although it's not much fun if one is a chicken, seeing your mates disappear one by one and wondering when it's your turn. It's like 'death row' without appeal.

As the day wears on I can't decide if this shopping trip is a 'reccy' or an attempt to purchase. Which man is clever enough to predict what a woman in shopping mode is thinking? I'm not, but in the end it proves to be a 'reccy' with a few definite 'maybes' thrown in. Pleased with her day so far Nettie decides that we will walk back to the hotel. Along the way we pass the main taxi ranks in a square that looks as though it could have been a bus station in a former life with raised kerbstones in lines to keep some semblance of order. It's hard to tell, as all of the buildings and roads are less than fifty years old. Looking at some of the buildings time has not been kind to them. We see a feral kitten that is still pink and probably only a few days old curled up on a pavement. I wonder what its chances of survival are. We walk past the football stadium and that does look to be built to a high standard with a playing surface to match. Further on we pass some more shops and stalls selling all the same stuff that we have seen in the souk. I am now on the limit of my patience for shopping and so to give myself a reward for not 'losing it' I go into the travel agents opposite the hotel to book myself a half-day trip to another town. I am told that there are not enough people to organise one yet but if I leave my details with him he will get back to me. I'm still waiting!

Back at the hotel, something that we have noticed from our bedroom is the beautiful sunsets, but the balcony is in the wrong place for a good picture. With that in mind I grab my camera and head for the beach to take a shot. I know that it takes four minutes from the time the sun touches the horizon until it disappears because I've timed it. I take several shots and while I am making my way back a man on a bicycle stops me and asks if I want to buy some marijuana. I decline and wonder if that is what is meant by pedalling drugs! Just as I am laughing at that thought I see another man piling a load of paintings on to the back of his moped, to take home for the night, knowing that he will return tomorrow and display them all over again.

For our evening meal we pick a fish restaurant for yet another superb meal. I have now got into the habit of only having a main meal and a drink, after eating most of the olives and bread that come out as appetisers. Everywhere is still quiet. The restaurants are only a fraction full, which is not so good for them but for us it is ideal because we are assured of good service and attentive waiters.

I then overhear a man on another table telling his companions how to sex an elephant and he swears it is true.

'Stick your finger in some elephant droppings and then quickly insert that finger into your mouth, except with a magician's slight of hand you don't actually put that finger in your mouth but another finger. Make some slurping noises and say that by the taste of it, one can tell if it is male or female. The gullible actually insert the dirty finger in their mouth!'

Text to Junior: ***Went to souk. Walked miles. Took picture of sunset. Offered marijuana. Can now sex an elephant!***

14-11-12

It is 04-30 and the seagull is back. It has squawked loud enough to wake me, hoping that I might feed it breakfast. I don't and I won't. I go back to sleep instead. Nettie remains comatose. When she does eventually wake up it is to make a cup of tea and to rouse me gently. It is so much more of a civilised start than two days ago. Then the Dirham drops; we are going out on a quad bike and a 4x4 trip through a semi-desert area and she is excited. This is her way of curbing her excitement, making tea!

At breakfast we notice some new arrivals, which, are easy to pick out because of their pasty skin. We linger over an extra coffee and croissant until my attention is drawn to the omelette lady. Up until now I have been avoiding a cooked breakfast but once I see her I give in. She has sad eyes and I think that is what attracts me to her. They are not sad in the sense of being unhappy but sad in the sense of being resigned to her position in life. It seems like cooking omelettes is as good as it's going to get for her, that she has reached the pinnacle of her culinary expertise when deep down she knows that she can do better but has no idea how to proceed. I have an omelette, even though I don't really want one and I try to engage her in conversation, as do others in the queue in front of me, but it is obvious that it is something she is not encouraged to do, talk to the clientele. The omelette is fine though. I might try again tomorrow.

'When we've finished breakfast do you fancy a stroll along the beach?' asks Nettie.

'That will be lovely,' I say having been taken by

surprise at the suggestion.

'A stroll mind you, not a route march.'

'Of course.'

The stroll along the beach is relaxing. Strolling in the Atlantic Ocean is even better. It is a little on the cool side but it's the wave pattern that fascinates me. The water seems to retreat faster than the waves coming in which causes them to stop. After two or three waves have stacked up the weight of water wins the day and it all floods in covering 30 or 40 metres at a time. One has to be wary because walking in water that just covers the feet one minute becomes a knee-deep experience the next. I point out where I ventured on my own the previous day but Nettie decides that we ought to get back to the hotel because we don't want to be late for our semi-desert experience. We head for the promenade. No sooner have we put our sandals back on than the hawkers are trying to grab our attention but without success. Just outside the back of the hotel I do see something that grabs my attention – bicycle hire! I make a mental note that if tomorrow is going to be another day by the pool for Nettie then I am going to hire a bike for part of the day. I can usually manage part of a day by the pool but not the whole day, even less if the music is too loud. It disturbs my reading!

Her timing is spot on as usual as the transport arrives to take us to the area for our 4x4 and quad bike experience. Thirty minutes later we are at the side of the road outside a wooden shed with the 4x4 and the bike ready for our use. Our guide takes the bike while Nettie and I take the 4x4. We are kitted out with hairnets, helmets, goggles and a facemask to keep the dust out. Off we go, slowly at first, with the guide constantly checking up on us. As he can see that we are reasonably proficient the speed increases. Bombing through the red dust is great fun, churning up the dirt, taking hills and slopes in our stride and noting that the vegetation is getting more and more sparse. We stop and swap over several times, to give us both some experience on the bike. When it comes to my turn on the bike I have to negotiate a rock covered dusty lane bordered with cacti. Any mistake here will be nasty. Thankfully I survive to tell the tale.

Halfway through our afternoon of fun on four wheels we stop in the middle of nowhere at a small dwelling where we are treated to a light Moroccan snack. It is a simple affair with bread to dunk in three different dips. One is olive oil, another is honey and a third is peanut butter with argan oil. A few sweet biscuits follow along with Moroccan tea. Then the small talk begins and football is a keen topic. However, the accent that the Moroccans use when speaking French is difficult to follow but player's names transcend all language barriers and accents. Like all football conversations we don't agree on some aspects of the game but we don't fall out over it either.

After a very pleasant break it's back to the 4x4 and quad bike.

'Can I drive this last bit?' asks Nettie, who is having the time of her life.

'Certainly,' I reply even though I want to because it's brilliant fun. I also need to get some brownie points!

Nettie drives over what proves to be the toughest section of all. As the guide has seen how capable we are he takes us off the marked track in places and down some truly steep hills, which Nettie excels in negotiating. She is having a great time and riding shotgun is an interesting experience especially when I try to line up a photo shot! We manage at one point, to ride through an area where a goat herder is rounding up his animals with the help of his dogs but they take more interest in us than in herding the goats much to his annoyance. It is but a brief moment of time and then they disappear in our red dust as we pull away.

Eventually we make it back to the starting point after a truly wonderful afternoon. Our clothes are cleaned off with the airline that is normally used to inflate tyres but nothing is going to blow away the memories from our best experience so far.

Text to Junior: ***Walked in the Atlantic. Quad biked in the desert. Best day so far.***

15-11-12

The seagull is back; again! This time it wakes me at 04-00 but it doesn't stay long, just long enough to wake me up and then disappear. I think it's revenge for not getting fed. I think about reading for a while but the light from the bedside lamp is so poor that I resort to using a head torch. It's either that, or sit on the toilet in the bathroom where the light is so much better. If I take the second course of action and Nettie discovers me, she will then ask what I'm doing and if I tell her that I've been woken up by a seagull and can't get back to sleep, it wouldn't sound very convincing. I suspect that her first course of action would be to check the level in the vodka bottle! As it is I get back to sleep for another three hours before starting the day properly. Predictably enough Nettie declares over breakfast that she will spend the morning by the pool so I declare that I am hiring a bike for four hours. Part of her worries about what I'll get up to and part of her can't wait to hear about it!

I make my way to the man with the bike, at the back of the hotel. He is a tall, slim, elderly gent in Berber dress and a beard. He speaks excellent English as well as French and is kind enough to draw me a map of how to get to the next town, which is ten kilometres away. He wishes me good luck and gives me a cycle lock, should I stop somewhere for a drink. It's great to be back on two wheels again. The cycling conditions are perfect. There is very little breeze, the temperature is in the mid-twenties and because of the French influence in Morocco, there are cycle lanes. Apart from that cycling on pavements is acceptable.

I recognise all the first part of the route from yesterday when we were driven to the shed to start our 4x4 experience. There the familiarity ends as I turn off at the junction that will take me to Ingezane just a short distance further on. It is as the bike man said, 'very local, no criminality and very safe'. This is not a town for tourists but one they pass through. I cycle round some of the streets and it looks like a lot of the area is a 'work in progress' even though it's finished. Road junctions are great fun even though I probably take the longest way round a roundabout but I figure that it's better to be safe than sorry.

Having seen what I came to see, and it was as I was told, not touristy, I head back with the intention of photographing things on the way. However curiosity gets the better of me and I sidetrack myself by exploring side roads. The first diversion takes me to an area where there are children hanging around on street corners looking like they have time to spare. Ever mindful of my experience in Gambia when I was held hostage and only released on payment of a small fee, I have no intention of being their amusement for the day so I turn back and continue along the main road again. Outside of the Navy headquarters I stop and wait for a lorry to cross in front of me to allow it to enter through the gate but before that can happen a guard moves me on and makes the lorry wait! At the next turning on my right I go exploring again and find a thriving community around the town square where the kerbstones have been put in place but no tarmac has been laid on either the road or the square. I watch a policeman as he walks down a narrow road where a market is in full swing but I don't follow, as the crowd is so dense between the stalls that there is no room for the bike. I turn round again, rejoin the main road and then cycle along the road that divides the tourist part of Agadir from the local part. The scenery is becoming familiar now as the hill that we were driven up on the first day comes into view. If I continue along it I will end up in the next town in the opposite direction from where I've just been. Instead I turn left and cycle into the fishing port, where I failed to get to, when out on my first walk. I head for a space between two huts when a uniformed man directs me away from that route and indicates that I should go past his hut on the other side. I do as I'm told. I cycle along an empty road, come to a military establishment, turn round and head for the quay. There is little activity going on but the boats are unbelievably rusty. I wouldn't fancy being out at sea in any of them. Further on there are dozens of smaller open craft and men on the quayside sorting out their nets. Part of the scene looks almost biblical. From here, I make my way back to the huts in order to leave the docks only to be confronted by a sign, which translated says, 'Customs Stop'. I have no passport or any form of identification on me and I am on a hired bicycle. The vehicle in front of me is an orange town taxi and he has been stopped. In a moment of bravado I decide to keep cycling and chance my luck. I pass the hut, go round the taxi and never look back. I just keep on pedalling. Fortunately nobody pursues me. From here I think about looking into the area where the fish restaurants are but decide against it as all the mornings catch have been sorted and accounted for and the restaurants are busy grilling for all they are worth.

I now decide to cycle the whole length of the promenade to see if I've missed anything. When I've covered about three-quarters of the entire length I notice a stunning looking girl posing for pictures at the water's edge. She is posing in a very professional way and it takes all of my attention. However I fail to notice, until the very last minute, that I am heading straight for a lamppost. Fortunately I see it just in time and narrowly avoid it, but in doing so almost clatter into a street trader! I complete the cycle then turn back and find the ice cream stall. It is the best ice cream that I have tasted outside of Italy.

My time is up, my backside is numb but the four hours have been just wonderful. The traffic was more considerate to cyclists than at home and so it is with a heavy heart that I give my bike back. Thinking ahead at the possibility of hiring the bike again I go and purchase a map.

Nettie is fully rested, browning nicely and is ready to go shopping again. We spend a couple of hours looking around and when she wonders where we are, I am able to draw on my experience of wandering to tell her. I think the whole experience of walking and cycling is helping me to orientate myself because I am a lot slower at 'knowing where I am' than my good lady is, who has a built in sense of positioning.

Text to Junior: ***40km bike ride. Upset military. Jumped customs. Just another quiet day in the sun.***

16-11-12

Today is overcast, so we linger over breakfast chatting to a Welsh couple that always make a point of speaking to us at the beginning of the day. We refer to it as our de-briefing session. Today, however, it lasts until lunchtime. The waiters are getting anxious because they have cleared every other table and set them ready for lunch and here we are still sitting at our breakfast table. When we do leave and go our separate ways, they pounce quickly to clear up so there is no chance that we could get back to the table even if we wanted to. Looking back, we were just being inconsiderate.

We wander along the street at the front of the hotel and decide to go on the tourist train around town. While we are waiting, we get chatting to an American with a Moroccan wife who is from Casablanca. They have two children and the eldest says that he wishes he could be in England so that he can speak English all the time and not have to put up with all the foreign languages that he faces on a daily basis. We discuss all manner of topics with them like Area 51 and whether the moon landings really happened. He says that he loves the British sense of humour and particularly likes the TV programmes like *Fawlty Towers* and *Butterflies.*

The train comes in and we part company. We board at the rear while they board at the front. Part of the way round a lady in front of me turns round and asks me if I will take a picture of her and her husband. I take her camera and think about asking her to smile, but don't, because she is wearing a burka. I know she is smiling though, because the eyes are the give away. It's easy to curl ones mouth up at the corners and pretend, but a true smile starts with the eyes and the mouth follows naturally. She is definitely smiling. I take the picture. She thanks me, then turns back to carry on chatting to her husband.

When the tour has gone full circle Nettie's ego is fully charged as her blonde hair has attracted winks, smiles and waves from every red-blooded male within sight, especially those in uniform! I feel that she encourages it with her flirtatious behaviour. She doesn't deny it. From the train we make our way through the zoo and I am able to give a partially guided tour as I was here a few days earlier. Nettie has it in mind just to wander and see if she can discover some hitherto unseen attraction. There aren't any, at least there aren't for me. For her there is the sight of a man stripping off naked in the street and then dressing again before walking nonchalantly away. Everywhere we look we can't see any women on the street or in the cafes; they are all men.

For our evening meal we go back to the restaurant that I have no recollection of leaving after feeding the cat. There is entertainment on the menu tonight. The staff greet us warmly so I must have behaved myself that night. The food is every bit as good as last time and when the musicians come amongst the diners one of them heads straight for someone sitting along side of me at the next table, hoping to get him on stage. He makes all manner of gestures but this man will not budge. I think something must have got lost in translation because he is convinced that it is Moroccan foreplay and he wants no part of it, at least that's what he tells me later! The musician then tries his luck with me. He wants me to put his hat on and spin the tassel. I try but I don't have the knack, instead I tell him, via a series of gestures that I want to play with his finger symbols. He understands and lets me play them. I place them on my fingers, pick up the rhythm and follow him onto the stage. I play, I dance and I keep the rhythm at the same time as doing squat jumps like a Cossack dancer. I leave the stage to loud applause.

Nobody follows me. The entertainment continues and we enjoy a great evening.

Text to Junior: *Quiet day. Raucous evening. Played in a Moroccan band. Record contract imminent!*

17-11-12

At breakfast Nettie looks lovingly into my eyes and says, 'Do you know what I plan to do today?'

'What's that dearest?'

'Shopping in the souk.'

'Again!'

'What do you mean "again"? I didn't buy anything last time.'

'Is it compulsory to buy?' I ask.

'You just don't understand do you?'

I don't answer. I've learned not to question too much the female theory of shopping, especially Nettie's.

'Our time in Agadir is coming to an end and I haven't bought enough things yet.'

'What about......'

I don't get to finish the sentence as Nettie gives me one of those looks that tell me to quit before she gets cross. I can tell she is getting agitated because the other day when we were looking and she didn't actually buy anything it goes down as a failure in her book. Now she has a chance to put it right. Unfortunately it is raining and our departure for the souk is delayed. Nettie is getting impatient.

Eventually the rain eases off, we make our way to the souk and she is off, a woman on a mission. It's hard to keep pace with her. Her first purchase is a pair of lightweight shoes and when haggling the price she tries to swap her old ones for the new ones. It doesn't work. Then she tries part exchange; that doesn't work either. Moving on, we see a shoemaker at work and the smell of adhesive is overpowering. In England glue sniffing is a crime but here in the souks of Agadir it is an occupational hazard! Nettie covers as many stalls as she can and when she's satisfied that there really isn't anything else that she can buy that she can realistically carry home, we leave. I buy some figs, just to break the boredom of trying to look interested.

After the marathon shopping expedition we go for a therapeutic stroll along the beach. We can see where the rain has run through the drainage system under the promenade and washed away the sand in certain places, exposing the rocks below. The hotel beach areas have obviously been well thought out, as they now stand on sand plateaux, unaffected by the surrounding erosion. I'm not sure who the therapy is for. Is it for me for keeping my cool during a day of shopping or for my happily contented wife who has now made a considerable contribution to the local economy?

For our evening meal we return to the same restaurant that we were in last night and the same musicians are on stage again. The one who had let me play with his finger symbols knows I am here but refuses to make eye contact. Instead it is left to a drummer to circulate among the crowd of diners. Eventually he gets to me and I am allowed to play the drum. Others have gone before me and others follow, but the highlight for the diners is the presentation of a birthday cake to a table behind us. The cake is presented with sparklers, where we might have candles. The traditional song is played and sung, followed by applause and the cutting of the cake. It's a great moment for them and for us, seeing a local family of several generations all out celebrating together.

By now Nettie has trained the waiter to bring her a pot of boiling water and a jug of cold milk so that she can make her own tea. He cannot understand this strange English custom but goes along with it anyway. I settle for another bottle of Moroccan beer for no better reason than I like to support the local economy. Nettie has her way and I have mine!

Text to Junior: ***Long day shopping. Played drums after dinner. C.D. out next week!***

18-11-12

Today we are supposed to meet up with the Invisible Man, our holiday rep, to confirm our transfer back to the airport but after two hours of waiting we give up. I hate being kept waiting by anyone. I am getting cross. Nettie tries to calm me by suggesting that we sit by the pool and relax. It is early afternoon by now and the music is as loud as ever which does nothing to placate me. The Russians are sunbathing standing up. Why do they do that? The exercise class is taking place but there's nobody joining in so the instructor performs on her own. Then comes the straw that breaks this particular camel's back. The records are Christmas ones, requesting that it snow! I have had enough. I turn to my darling wife who is lying down, quite contentedly, listening to the music and reading a book (how does she do that?) and tell her in harsher tones than I intend, 'Darling I'm going for a walk.'

'Why?' she asks me looking perplexed.

'The music volume is at the limit of my tolerance but when they start on the Christmas stuff and want snow when it's still November and the temperature is in the mid 20's, I mean, that is just too much!'

'But it's nearly Christmas dear.'

'It's November!' I say emphatically at which point the volume is turned up a notch. The aerobics instructor still has no takers so I expect this is her revenge. Crank up the volume and make sure no one can do anything except watch or join in. In my case I've got a third option; I'm going for a walk!

'See you later darling,' I say and off I go, leaving the excessive noise behind. This time I decide to head inland and see how far I can go. I walk round the gardens, when the quicker option would be to walk through them and then up a hill. Ahead of me is a collection of buildings, which from where I am standing, looks like the worst excesses of inner city development back home. I turn left and walk along the side of one of the better made roads. When the pavement stops I continue on into the sparse surroundings, thinking that I might be on my way to my own forty days in the wilderness. It doesn't help matters when I see dogs on the loose or a man picking his way through a communal rubbish bin. Further on I feel a stone wedge itself between the bottom of my foot and the top of my sandal, which causes me some discomfort. It is one of life's mysteries for me. How does it happen? I try to shake it free but on the opposite side of the road and going in the same direction as I am, is a middle-aged man dressed in Berber clothing, rattling a plastic bag. The noise makes me look up and I see that he is smiling. It has an unsettling affect on me, so I give up and limp on. A dozen steps later the stone is still hurting so I stop and shake my leg again to try and get rid of it. He rattles his bag again while looking straight at me! I think about undoing my sandal and doing the job properly but as I am about to, he looks set to cross the road and join me. Fortunately he is prevented from doing so by a passing car. I'm not going to risk it again so I have one last vigorous shake and apart from putting a huge smile on his face it does actually free the stone from my foot. Grateful for that I hasten on. I have a furtive backward glance and see that the plastic bag man has gone back to his slow silent shuffle, looking crestfallen because I suspect that he feels that I have somehow teased him with a bit of leg wangling that may have a different meaning out here. Maybe that is why the man in the restaurant refused to answer the call of the musicians the other night.

My mind is racing now. Thinking back to the other day when we saw a man strip off in the street and then get dressed again, there were no women to be seen, so what do the males do here for excitement? Strip off in the street, or get excited by a bit of leg wangling or chat up male diners? They never ask the women. I could be vulnerable out here in the wilderness on my own so I move on.

I turn left again and head along a dual carriageway without footpaths, an interesting experience! My destination is the port. As I get nearer, I wonder if I ought to take another, closer look at the quayside but decide not to because I feel I've had enough excitement for one day without the risk of becoming a fisherman's friend as well!

So I head back to the promenade and catch the sting of sand being blown off the beach. I decide that if Man Friday had walked along here today Crusoe would never have found him. The windy blast doesn't last long. I stop for an ice cream, only to get pestered by a child begging me to buy him one. I tell him to go away because he is clean, well dressed and just trying his luck, whereas if he had been dressed in rags, looking dirty and hungry that may have weakened my resolve. The trouble is that if you give in to one of them the next thing you know is that you have attracted a crowd, become like the Pied Piper and get pestered forever and a day.

Further on another man stops me and insists on giving me his business card. I decline but he is insistent.

'Where you from in England?' he asks me.

'Isle of Man,' I lie.

Obviously he has never heard of the Isle of Man because the next thing he says is, 'My girlfriend Pakistani, she lives in Leeds. We get married next year. Come in my shop. It's free.'

'Come in my space, you get fat lip.' I growl quietly. I wish him well and walk on, quickly.

It is getting tiresome fending off these people and I'm glad to get back to the hotel after my little escapade. The music is still belting out but the Christmas play list has finished, as have the exercise classes, and the Russians are still standing. Nettie is nowhere to be seen so I go to our room. I find her there sipping tea and looking as contented as I've ever seen her.

'Have a good walk dear?' she enquires.

'I did. Would you like to hear about it?'

'Not now; tell me over dinner.'

I do, but gloss over some of the details. The steak with mushroom sauce that we have is the meal of the week so far.

Text to Junior: ***Quiet day. Went for a walk.*** No point worrying him!

19-11-12

At breakfast we are aware of some more new arrivals. A pair that catch my eye are French; she is tall, slim and seductive and for all the world looks like the cat that got the cream. He looks knackered. It looks like it could be an affair that she is enjoying but he realises he has more than he can handle. She plays with her food in a suggestive manner; he has lost his appetite. Oh how the imagination paints a picture!

Back in our room we find that the safe has stopped working. We report it to reception and they deal with it straight away. It is a battery malfunction and easily put right. It helps to pass the time until the Invisible Man is supposed to make himself known to us and tell us about our trip back to the airport. He doesn't show again but we do find someone who does sort it out for us. It's enough to drive a Muslim to drink or make a vicar swear!

Down by the pool the decibel level is as high as ever so I go for another walk, only a short one this time, along the promenade to the King's beach and back. On the way I am pestered so many times that I decide to return via the road and use only a small section of the promenade and see how many hawkers I can avoid. My yellow hat is proving a blessing and a curse. Those who have tried their luck and failed leave me alone but those who have not seen me before view me as a possible customer. Suddenly I am everybody's friend. I have more mates than Richard Branson but they can't decide if I'm French, German or English. I can ignore them in any language.

I make it back to the hotel and find Nettie all set to have a last splash in the Atlantic surf, so I turn round and go with her. I point out the sand erosion from the other day but she ignores me. Nettie is concentrating on trying out her new camera with different settings while photographing the waves. Eventually, having exhausted all possible setting combinations we return to the hotel via the promenade. I have one last encounter with a hawker who is trying to sell a rock with sparkly bits inside it. He is probably younger than he looks, has a few teeth missing, (I wonder why) and speaks very little English. He is rather too persistent for me so in the end I tell him that I bought one yesterday from his brother and have no need of another. That confuses him because it is not an answer he is used to. In fact I think it goes beyond his range of English vocabulary. He has become linguistically challenged. All he does is laugh at my remark and say, 'Yes, yes, very cheap, brother, yesterday, very good, ha ha, very cheap.'

That is as much as we hear as we walk out of earshot.

As it's our last night we feel that we ought to have one last tagine, to finish the holiday as we started it. We have beef with vegetables. The meat crumbles, it is that tender, the vegetables are tasty and I decide not to have a whole bottle of wine to myself, so I settle for a Moroccan beer. It is a good end to a pleasant break although I can't get over how quiet it is everywhere.

Text to Junior: ***Last full day. Went for a quiet walk. Have more mates than Richard Branson. Will text when we land.***

20-11-12

I don't like last days. The time drags because there is not much to do. Cases have to be packed, which doesn't take long when travelling on hand luggage as I do, and rooms have to be vacated. So we linger over breakfast and 'people watch'. The French lovers are lost in each other's gaze, oblivious to the outside world. We have a final de-briefing session with the Welsh couple and then my morning entertainment turns up in the unlikely form of ten year old Herman the chubby German. He is self assured and quite independent about sorting out his breakfast. He manages; somehow, to get his baguette stuck in the toaster and causes sparks to fly when he retrieves it with a bread knife. Just a couple of swift prods do the trick. German efficiency must be inbuilt; he has a natural born talent. I look at the omelette lady one last time and her sad eyes haven't changed. She still goes about her chores mechanically, doesn't smile, hardly ever speaks and seems as resigned as ever to her position in life.

'Have you enjoyed Agadir?' I ask my good lady.

'I certainly have. How about you?'

'I've enjoyed the warmth of the sun and being away from the cold of home but I haven't enjoyed it as much as Marrakech. I feel it's too European here whereas Marrakech is more Moroccan. Am I making any sense?'

'I know what you mean. I've had a lovely time, doing nothing. It has done me a power of good. The pool was excellent.'

'Don't get me started on the pool! The music was too loud; the play list was not to my liking, which is why I went out and about. I had great fun doing that.'

'What about all the encounters you had?'

'All part of the fun my dear; I don't go looking for

them, they just happen.'

'If you say so. Come on the bus is here. It's time to go.'

We don't chat too much on the way to the airport as we are thinking about the relative cold that awaits us at Gatwick. The flight is twenty minutes early arriving, thanks to a tail wind.

Text to Junior: ***Arrived home. All is well.***

Text from Junior: ***Excellent news. Welcome to England. Land of hope and glory.***

It is the first text and only text that I have received from him the entire holiday. I phone him when we arrive indoors.

'Hello Junior, we're back. Why didn't you respond to any of my text messages?'

'Because it's Africa,' he says in less than complimentary tones.

'So?'

'It's Africa,' he repeats with more emphasis on the "Africa". 'I don't know why anyone wants to go to Africa. I don't and I certainly won't send text messages there. You never know which tree they'll bounce off or who will read them, that's if they can read and if there are any trees left. It's Africa!' he repeats as though repeating it was enough of an explanation for his xenophobia.

I am flabbergasted at his outburst. Then, as a parting shot he says, 'Princess has asked me to ask you if you'd like to come to dinner on Sunday because she wants to hear all about it. I've told her it's Africa but she insists, so see you Sunday.' And with that he hangs up.

New Years Eve

Fed up with no decisions being made at our family lunches, Junior and Princess arrive, unexpectedly, on our doorstep. Nettie and I are surprised to see them, although we shouldn't be, as they have a habit of turning up unannounced. Junior who is in an unusually loquacious mood speaks first, 'Come on you two, we are going to the Indian restaurant for a meal and the table has been booked.'

I look at Nettie hoping for some sort of signal that this has been arranged behind my back but nothing is forthcoming.

'Well come on, time is pressing,' he insists.

Fortunately we have entertained this scenario before and are ready to go at short notice. Nettie would have preferred longer to prepare herself but she does what she calls a 'quick change'. To my untrained masculine eye the preparation looks good to me whether she takes ten minutes or ten hours, but I mustn't say that out loud.

'What's the occasion?' I ask Junior.

'It's New Years Eve and we have no travel plans for next year, so it might be a good time to start getting serious about it,'

'Fair enough.'

We arrive by taxi at the local Indian restaurant and see that it is busy. The waiters are going as fast as they can but I feel they are struggling a bit. We are shown to our table; order our meal and wait. A bottle of wine soon gets emptied and another ordered, then the popadoms arrive. Junior is still in jocular mood and tries to catch the waiter's eye to order some more lime pickle. The waiters are not playing ball; they are too busy on other tables. Junior's patience runs out, so he pulls out his mobile phone and phones the restaurant that we are now sitting in. The barman answers the call.

'Could we have some lime pickle on table seven please?' he asks.

I am looking at the barman, who seems bemused by the request and then looks in our direction. He can see who has called him, beams a broad smile and summons a waiter, telling him to deliver some more lime pickle to table seven. He does. Fortunately everyone in the restaurant can see what's going on, have heard the conversation and burst out laughing, including the people at the table that have momentarily lost their waiter. Thereafter the staff keeps a close eye on us!

We finish the meal, which is one of the best we've ever had locally and then make our way to the beach to let off some Chinese lanterns to celebrate the New Year. We watch as they drift out to sea on the gentle breeze. It is warmer than we might have expected and I feel a sense of optimism in the air. Normally the first thing that happens as the clock ticks into the New Year is that someone will ask the question, 'What New Year resolutions are you going to make?' It doesn't happen, which surprises me, but I've already made up my mind about two things. Firstly I'm not going to tell anyone what I'm going to do and secondly I've made my mind up to start on my list of city breaks. For years I have said that I would like to go here or I would like to go there but procrastination usually wins the day. This year will be different, I am going to try and live by a sign that I saw in Bologna on a short visit there. It said 'Carpe Diem'. Not knowing what it meant at the time I found out when I returned home and so that is the motto for the year, 'Seize the day' which is the modern translation of the phrase.

Budapest

In my haste to book this four-day break back in January I had overlooked the fact that it is Junior's birthday on the day we return, which doesn't go down too well with Nettie or Junior. So the suggestion is that we go to the Higham point-to-point meeting the week before, as we can't do anything together on the weekend nearest to his birthday because Nettie and I will be in Budapest.

My track record of picking winners at a racetrack is woeful. The rest of the family wait until I have made a selection, then avoid that horse like the plague. It has been said that I couldn't pick the winner in a one horse race! We drive the short distance to Higham, park up close to the track and immediately Junior says, 'What are you going to pick for the first race?'

'Wait and see,' I tell him.

He doesn't have long to wait. My fancied horse, the one I am backing to help change my fortunes pulls up having covered less distance than I have getting from the on-course bookmaker to the trackside!

'It was that one wasn't it?' he says, barely keeping a straight face. 'What are you going to pick in the second race?'

'Wait and see,' I say to him, feeling that things can't get any worse. They do.

The second horse is so frisky it tries to get to the start line by going the wrong way round the track! Eventually the jockey persuades the horse to go the right way and it does at least finish – well down the field.

The mirth continues, at my expense, so come the third race I try to save face by backing an odds on favourite. The winning of some money isn't important now, as it will be so little given the odds, that I just want to have the satisfaction of backing a winner. One bookmaker isn't even taking bets on the horse, he is that certain it will win, he offers odds for that horse and the second horse together. He even has odds of 40-1 for the favourite to be the only finisher. What can possibly go wrong?

The horse runs well, and as other horses drop out of the race, one by one, my jockey does a great job steering his mount through the field. All is going to plan until on the final run-in he is out-sprinted by the second favourite! More hoots of derision come my way, my lack of success continues and so I give up betting for the day. No bad run lasts forever I tell myself; it just seems that way while it's happening. And so on to Budapest and trying to check-in online.

For one and a half hours I try to accomplish the feat only to be told by the website that I have made an error. I check, re-check and check again and still I have no luck. I check my bank statement to make sure that I have paid for the trip and found that I have. I fill the form in again for the umpteenth time and still the error notice pops up.

By this time my composure is getting a little frazzled because I had wanted to have the task completed before Nettie comes in from work. I fail. As she walks through the door I explain what I've been trying to do and very calmly she tells me to try again while she stands and watches me. Unbelievably on the second attempt I manage to complete the mission.

'How do you do that?' I ask her.

'Do what?'

'Stand watch over me and see me do all the same things that I've been doing for the last ninety minutes only to have the error sign flash up and yet when you watch me I get straight through!'

'The site was probably busy,' she says matter of factly.

'Then why don't they flash up a sign to inform the user that the site is busy, instead of telling them that they've made an error. It causes people like me to doubt their own judgement when all along it isn't my fault at all!'

'Never mind dear, you've done it now,' she says rather patronisingly.

I just hate it when that happens. But I do manage to get the transport fixed up for getting to and from Stansted airport without any hassle, so fingers crossed it all works out well.

06-04-13

Junior turns up on time and drives us to the airport and after clearing formalities we have a cake and a coffee. I check the departure board and see that it is now time for us to make our way to Gate 7. Along the way I have a nagging suspicion that something is wrong. It is far too quiet. Upon arrival those suspicions are confirmed and it is indeed the wrong gate. I explain the problem to an Easyjet lady who makes a phone call and a world-weary, sixty-something year old man with silver hair and glasses comes along and is instructed to take us via a short cut to Gate 42, where we need to be. My only consolation at having made another mistake is that apart from us, he has to drive four young men to another gate, who are bound for Glasgow and another man bound for a destination that I didn't hear. Three separate cases of a wrong gate sounds suspicious to me and I am still not sure that I did mis-read the board, but with my recent track record of mistakes I have to go along the route of probability and say that I may have done. Are the others as bad as me I wonder?

The driver has seen it all before and after he drops them off I ask him, 'Does this happen often, with people getting to the wrong gate?'

'All the time, every day,' he says in a bored sounding tone.

'So we're not alone in getting it wrong then?'

'Not at all, at least you're at the correct airport. I had a businessman here the other day who had been caught speeding, doing over 100mph on the M25, and he asked me if I could get him to his flight as he only had fifteen minutes to spare. I asked him for his boarding pass, took one look at it and said "not a chance". He started to get annoyed with me until I asked him if he had read his boarding pass properly and then told him that this was Stansted and he should have been at Heathrow. He said that he always flew from Stansted and I told him that this time he wasn't, so while he drives back he should think on how to manage his life without a car with the inevitable ban that will follow getting caught driving at such an excessive speed and also to read his ticket properly next time.

Then there was the couple that had arranged to meet in the coffee shop. He phoned her and said that he had arrived and asked where she was, she said that she was in the coffee shop, as arranged, but couldn't see him. It turned out that it was the same chain of coffee shops but he was sitting in Stansted whereas he should have been with her at Gatwick!

I've seen it all here, I could tell you stories like that all day long.'

By now we have arrived at Gate 42 and after taking a short cut up the stairs we are in time to join the queue that has just begun to board the plane.

'Just think dearest, if I hadn't mis-read that board, and I'm still not sure that I did, we would never have got to hear those stories or been given a tour of the airport would we?'

Judging by the frosty look I am given I should have kept quiet!

The flight to Budapest is punctual and as we make our way through the airport I go and book the shuttle bus to take us to the hotel. Ever mindful of my catalogue of misfortunes of late I deliberately check with the receptionist, three times, that she has booked the correct hotel. She speaks perfect English, so I have no doubts that she has indeed booked everything correctly. Within ten minutes the driver arrives and we are on our way. As we close in on the centre of Budapest I am getting excited that the weekend is about to begin. Just as soon as I have experienced that euphoric moment my heart sinks when the driver crosses over the River Danube and deposits us outside a hotel and tells us that we have arrived.

'It's the wrong hotel,' I protest.

'Ticket,' he demands in a brusque manner.

He looks at it and then points out that the ticket the lady has given me is for the hotel we are now outside and not the one that we are staying in. While I stand there, stunned by the news, he swiftly departs, leaving us in Buda when we should be in Pest. I yell in frustration, cursing my run of bad luck and wondering when my fortunes will change. This latest episode is nothing more than two hotels with very similar sounding names but with different spellings and I have been given the wrong one. Then a strange calmness comes over me as I think that maybe now a line has been drawn under it all, as this is the third piece of misfortune to have happened for this trip. First there was the bother with checking in on-line, secondly there was the matter of the wrong departure gate and now this; the wrong hotel and we haven't even reached the right one yet!

For some strange reason I feel that I know where I am even though I have never been to Budapest before. We walk over the Chainlink Bridge into Pest and hire a taxi to take us the two miles to the hotel. We have arrived at last. The man on the reception desk is a revelation with his information about what to do, where to go and he makes us feel most welcome. He recommends a nearby restaurant that serves authentic Hungarian food and he will gladly book us a table should we choose to go. We agree and then make our way to our room on the second floor.

'It's better than the one you booked in Carcassonne, I'll give you that,' says Nettie.

'Things are looking up then,' I venture.

'Could have been closer to the city centre,' she replies.

'One thing at a time,' I say, defending my position.

We settle into our room, which is clean, tidy and basic. There are no outside windows as everything is built round a quadrangle with the inner part on floor one being the dining area. The air conditioning works, the water is hot, it's all looking good. After a short rest we go in search of the restaurant that we have been booked into.

The five-minute walk takes us half an hour as we miss a turning and I'm not taking the blame this time! When we do arrive at the small establishment, off the beaten track near a corner of a quiet side road, we are welcomed at the door and shown to our table, noting on the way two musicians, one guitarist and one violin player. They play soft background type music that encourages a few couples to get up and waltz their way around the tables. It feels like we have stepped back in time to the era of romantic black and white films. While we soak up this pleasant change from the modern piped music we continue the Hungarian theme by having a mixture of Hungarian food, including goulash, which is now just a tourist dish. It tastes bland but is edible and we spend the next two hours avoiding making eye contact with the musicians as we plan what we are going to do tomorrow. Once we have sorted it out we head back to the hotel for an early night and this time we do get it right. It only takes us five minutes to walk the distance.

I try my key in the door but it doesn't work so I go downstairs to reception and get it re-programmed. I had made the mistake of putting the electronic key next to my mobile phone, which somehow causes the key to not work. I've had the same thing happen with train tickets not working the barriers at stations back home. After such a reasonably restful day I feel strangely tired and fall sound asleep in no time at all.

07-04-13

At 01-00 the loudest snoring I've ever heard from Nettie in over 30 years of married life wakes me up. I feel sure there will be complaints from neighbouring rooms. I can hear them when they flush the toilet or use the shower, so goodness knows how loud the noise is that they can hear. I can't even escape to a spare room! I try earplugs but they are totally useless against such a racket. I'm sure sleeping next to a road drill would be a quieter option but there's never one when you want one. In desperation I try to block out the noise mentally by imagining that I am lying on a tropical island with dusky maidens whispering sweet nothings in my ear. Just as the gossamer thin image is almost in place a new terrifying decibel-busting nasal hurricane blows the image away, leaving me adrift. I try again but with less success than before, as I am now half expecting the next blast. I give up and decide to read. I have no bedside light; there is only the one, and it isn't on my side of the bed. In a moment of brilliance, which I do have occasionally, I remember that I have my head torch with me, so put that in place and start reading.

Concentrating against such an intense noise is difficult and I think that the effort it entails has an affect. By 04-30 I think I have gone deaf and then I realise that the snoring has stopped. I am so relieved that I fall asleep in seconds, sleeping the sleep of the dead! It lasts until 08-45 when I wake up feeling shattered. It feels like I have been partying all night. If only! It has been a long night.

We descend one floor to the dining area. Nettie is as chirpy as a sparrow and wonders why I am so tired.

'It was your snoring. It was the loudest I've ever known it to be. I couldn't sleep and the little I did get, wasn't enough.'

'Oh good,' she beams, 'I feel fine, I slept wonderfully well and am already to explore the wonderful city of Budapest which is known as the Pearl of the Danube. It is made up of three small towns, Obuda, and Buda from the other side of the river and Pest on this side of the river. Did you know that?'

'Yes I did as a matter of fact,' I reply.

'In 1873 they merged and formed Budapest as it is today. Did you know that parts of the east and west banks are now listed as a UNESCO World Heritage Site?'

'No I didn't.'

'Come on, time for breakfast,' she enthuses.

I do as I'm told and although the buffet isn't the best we've ever eaten it's plenty good enough. Gradually the dining room fills up with students who are behaving exactly as I expect students to behave, in fact I think that looking around we are the only two who aren't students! A thought occurs to me in that we could have claimed a 'first' if the students had complained about too much noise coming from our room last night!

After breakfast we walk to the New York Café, a grand building with an even grander interior. It was built in 1894 and after a chequered history and lack of maintenance it was finally bought by an Italian and restored to its original glory in 2006. It is a fabulous place. It is called the most beautiful café in the world and it is easy to see why. We go in and are shown to a table by a waiter who places menus before us. As we have just eaten we settle for a couple of drinks, a hot chocolate with coconut and Baileys for Nettie and a pikans esipos kave chilivel for myself, which translates as a spicy coffee with chilli. We linger over the drinks as it is nippy outside with the temperatures, like at home, about ten degrees below what it should be at this time of year. The street thermometer is showing just 9°C.

Reluctantly we leave the palatial surroundings of the New York Café and buy tickets for the green and pink site-seeing buses and boat tours in a combined ticket that gives us unlimited travel for 48 hours. With that we are given a book of money off vouchers as well. Within minutes the green bus turns up and we hop on. The first place that grabs our attention is the Jewish Synagogue which is a tall colourful building and in the time it takes to slowly drive past it, listening to the audio commentary, I am ready to sign up for the Jewish Tour at another time on another visit even though I imagine it could be a harrowing experience with tales of persecution.

After the Synagogue we double back on ourselves and cross the River Danube, which is anything but the blue of the song and enter Buda. The bus climbs up the winding road past Gellert Hill and we alight at the Citadel Restaurant, where all the vendors of souvenirs are waiting for us. They are not pushy and are content to wait for us to approach them. The merchandise looks to be of a better quality than most that we have seen in other parts of the world and that in itself is a refreshing change.

The views are stunning or they would be if the mist had not cast a veil over them, yet there is just enough of a hint of the views to urge the photographer in me to come here again tomorrow if it is sunny. We hop on and off the green bus and the pink bus all day long before we eventually make it back to the riverbank in Pest where the boat trips depart from.

It is good to sit down, have a beer and take stock of the day while the throb of the diesel engine sends the boat up the river to circle Marshall Island before returning to the start point. It is a very pleasant hour taking in all the sites and in particular, as we pass under the bridges, to note just how well constructed they all are. It is all the more impressive when one considers that all the bridges over the Danube at Budapest were bombed during World War II. All have been restored to their former glory and in one case improved and renamed.

After the cruise we go to a nearby café for dinner and anybody brave enough to dine outside are given blankets to put around their knees. We are not that brave so eat inside. The temperature is dropping from chilly to cold, annoyingly so, and then we return to the river for the night time cruise. It follows a similar route to the earlier one but turns round before the island and goes further down the river in the opposite direction before returning to the berth. The river at night looks a different place with all the lights illuminating the bridges across the river and the many historic buildings along both banks of this World Heritage Site.

We decide to walk back the two miles to the hotel, taking our time and calling into a pub along the way at about the halfway point. It is quiet and, as far as I can tell, there are only four of us in the place. It is becoming a pleasant feature for me that Budapest in general is quiet. So far we haven't encountered any revellers or loud people and long may it continue!

Back inside our hotel we settle for an early night. As I lay in bed reading, I am aware of rumbling beneath the bed and realise that it is the metro passing through way below the hotel. The students are making a noise but unless they start being a nuisance, like causing damage to our room, or banging on the door and running then I am quite happy for them to continue.

08-04-13

Fortunately I sleep soundly until 05-30 when the snoring starts again. It is not as bad as last night, it is the same vibration but with a muffler on to deaden the harshness of the noise. However the experience of last night has left an imprint on my consciousness that is difficult to get rid of and so while the volume is less than before the fact that it is there at all is enough to deny me further sleep. With that in mind I decide to make use of the time by charging up the batteries for my camera and phone.

After breakfast I make my way to reception and ask the man behind the desk if he can sort out our return trip with the shuttle bus after I explain the mix-up to him. It is no sooner said than done. If only all problems could be sorted out as quickly. While I have his attention I ask him to call us a taxi to take us to Heroes Square, which he does. It is not a great distance but I feel that if we are going to be on foot as much as yesterday then I have to consider Nettie's ability to repeat what she did yesterday. Once at the landmark we pay the driver and are immediately approached by an Englishman.

'Can I interest you in the red bus tour?' he asks.

'No thanks, we're on the green bus route,' replies Nettie.

'Fair enough,' he replies. His reaction seems like he has heard the word "no" on more than one occasion, is quite used to it and takes no offence at our refusal.

'What's an Englishman doing selling bus tickets in Budapest?' I ask him.

'I met and married a Russian lady who lives in Hungary, which is where I now live, but we're getting divorced. I thought that she married me for a passport but she hates England so it wasn't that, it couldn't be for the money because she has more money than anyone I know. Maybe she actually liked me but she doesn't any more so we're getting divorced. She has taken my company though, which is why I've had to get a job to pay the bills until I can get something more permanent sorted out. Anyway, you two have a good day,' he ends up saying.

'Thank you,' I reply, 'and best of luck for the future.'

'Did you want to know his life history?' asks Nettie as we leave him and start to explore.

There are groups of schoolchildren or students, it is difficult to tell which, armed with notebooks and pens trying to jot down whatever bits of information come their way. As most places are closed on Mondays it gives us the chance to explore the outside of buildings and gardens of more places than we would otherwise have done, had we ventured inside. It also gives us places to earmark should we return to Budapest in the future.

After a couple of hours we hop on the bus and cross the Danube into Buda again and hop off at the Citadel to re-take some pictures that we had taken yesterday. The scene is so much better now that the mist has cleared. We look among the souvenir stalls and Nettie's eye is taken by a three-way game of chess that she thinks will be ideal for Junior's birthday present. I'm sure she's right. She has an uncanny knack of getting just the right present for whomever she is buying.

From there we make our way to the Fisherman's Bastion, where we spend the afternoon wandering around buildings, where the white stone is so well defined it would be easy to think that one has wandered into Disneyland by mistake. We go into the quadrangle of the Royal Palace and it does remind me a great deal of Buckingham Palace. Outside is the Matthias fountain, but sadly, no flowing water. The intricate bronze figurines, depicting a hunting scene, look in need of a clean as do all the other figures that we have seen in the city. Nearby is a building, left exactly as it was, with the walls pitted with bullet marks from an old conflict. Further on we see the Matthias church with its multi-coloured roof.

We milk the views for all they're worth as we make our way on foot down to the Adam Clark Square which is between the Chainlink Bridge and the Budapest Castle Hill Funicular. Adam Clark was the Scottish born engineer who oversaw the construction of the bridge, which was the first permanent bridge over the Danube, linking Buda and Pest. He also designed the Buda Tunnel at the Buda bridgehead to provide easy access to places in Buda behind the hill. The square is named after him. In it is the zero kilometre stone, which is the official, starting point for all road measurements in Hungary.

At every turn there is history. We walk over the Chainlink Bridge, as we did on our first day in Budapest, and this time I study it more closely. The design is quite clearly done to make it look like a bicycle chain. It is very clever in its concept.

Once we arrive back in Pest we stop for a drink and decide that after walking round the market we will have dinner in the oldest restaurant in Pest. It is easy to find and in the dimly lit interior we notice four musicians who look as though they are about to start playing. We are told that we have three quarters of an hour before they actually do start, which pleases Nettie no end!

On the wall above the table, that we are seated at; is a plaque showing the level of the floodwater from many years ago. If I stand up, the water level would have been above my head. On the Buda side of the river there are two roads along the bank that run parallel. If the river water reaches eight metres above normal the lower road is closed, if it reaches ten metres above normal then the upper road is affected. How that equates to the flatter, Pest side of the river I don't know but I suspect the damage will be considerably greater than that in Buda.

As this is our last night in Budapest we decide to 'push the boat out' and spoil ourselves. We both have an aperitif followed by a beef dish for Nettie and goose leg with cabbage and mash for me. It is the tenderest piece of goose that I have ever eaten. For dessert we have pear with red wine, ice cream and cream. Our chosen wine is rosé, which is a compromise, as Nettie prefers white and I prefer red but we both get on with rosé. The musicians have started playing cocktail music and when they start to move among the tables we take it as our cue to leave.

09-04-13

The students are loud again, carrying on until 02-15, but not even that can deaden the noise that I am trying to sleep next to. I feel sleep deprived and cold inside. Maybe I'm sickening for something.

After breakfast I pack my suitcase and just read. I don't venture out, which is most unlike me as I usually like to get the last bit of site seeing squeezed in before departure, but today I just don't feel like it.

At midday the shuttle bus arrives and takes us back to the airport. The road passes through some very bleak, all concrete areas, a world away from the city of splendour that we have just left a few miles behind. We are safely despatched after forty-five minutes and that gives us plenty of time to wander around the airport and look at the facilities. By chance we find a Chinese fast food outlet so indulge in a chicken and boiled rice dish for lunch. We are using the last of our Hungarian currency up and leaving all coins behind.

By the time we pass through security I know for sure that the only metal on my person is my wedding ring and the zip fly on my trousers. The alarm goes off so I guess that it is my turn to be the random frisk victim. I stand still and raise my arms in a resigned manner waiting for the inevitable cursory frisk but I am wrong. The male official squeezes all my limbs reaching in as far as is decently possible, then he places his hands inside my trousers and feels his way around my torso. Not content with that I have to turn my back on him while he does the same thing again. I feel that he is enjoying himself too much but what choice do I have but to let him continue? If I object there will be no telling as what darkened room he may take me to and tell me to strip off. The thought of seeing him slap on rubber gloves is all too much. By now he has finished fondling me and I am allowed to proceed, thankfully.

The flight back is smooth and punctual. Stansted airport is quiet and so we only take ten minutes from leaving the plane, passing through passport control and customs before getting out of the building and into our taxi. By 19-00 we are home. It has been a great weekend. I was pleasantly surprised at how polite the people were. Car drivers anticipated us crossing the road and would stop in advance rather than race us to the pedestrian crossing. Generally people were quiet.

We neither saw, nor heard, any loud groups of people involved in anti-social behaviour. It has left a lasting impression on us. It could have been warmer but there is nothing we can do about the weather. Maybe we'll return someday and explore some more of this fine city. Before we think about planning any more trips we have to check in with Junior and the rest of the family. It is time we all got together for another one of our long lunches.

Nice One Monaco Too

'I don't like being called Peewee, Grumpy. Can I be something else?'

'I don't like being called Grumpy because I'm not,' I reply.

'You've always been Grumpy.'

'Only because you couldn't say Grandpa when you were little; you tried to say it but it came out as "Grumpy" and everyone else started calling me that, including your little sister. Tell you what, how about a more grown-up name like PJ?'

'PJ? Oh that's cool. PJ and Grumpy. I like that. High five Grumpy.'

'High five PJ.'

Our hands smack together just ahead of a clap of thunder and a sudden downpour of rain. It ruins our barbeque and sends us all scurrying indoors. It is such a shame because it's rare enough these days that the extended family gets together for a meal, so when we do it becomes something of an occasion. Usually there are several conversations going on at once so there is a lot of talking and not much listening. That is my perception of proceedings but apparently decisions do get made and I'm told that I just don't keep up with it all, as I am soon to find out. Once we are all safely indoors and in the dry, Princess speaks, 'So Nice it is then.'

'Whose niece?' I ask.

'Not niece, Nice, south of France.'

'When was all this decided?'

'Just now while you were playing with the children.'

'Lovely, when are we going?'

'July 18th for a week; six nights, seven days.'

It seems that my input counts for very little these days as the next generation have all the answers, or so they think. After a lifetime of travelling I would have thought that I might be able to offer some sort of advice, but apparently not. It seems that the Internet is the answer to everything and the one thing they all swear by. With that in mind I now go armed with 'Plan B', which is a list of things to do if the usual dithering on decision-making occurs, and when we travel as a group it is bound to happen! As we are going to be staying on the coast then I'm sure the beach will feature heavily in the itinerary. I don't mind spending some time on the beach but not all of the time especially when there are other places to go and things to see. I have a feeling that I am going to need 'Plan B'.

18-07-13

We leave Gatwick on the 06-05 flight to Nice, which lands on time and truth be told I can't say anything about the flight because I slept most of the way. Once we clear formalities I make my first break from the ranks. The general opinion is that we should get the express bus for €6 to the old town whereas I favour the shuttle bus from terminal two to terminal one and then get the local bus for €1-50 or €1 if we buy a ten journey ticket for €10.

'It's too much hassle,' declares Junior.

'No it isn't,' I say as I walk off and go my own way.

'We'll meet you in the café at the end of the road where we are staying. It is called Granny's Salon de Thé,' he shouts after me.

I have a brief look around and as usual everyone is talking at once except Junior who has that worried look on his face again. I've probably caused him to look like that more than anyone else! I am determined to prove a point and prove it I will.

I catch the shuttle bus to terminal one, go into the ticket office and purchase a ten journey ticket for €10. I then proceed to stand six where the number 23 bus is already waiting. I am unsure which stop to get off at and the bus driver is no help, so I eventually make an executive decision, pick a stop and make my way to the tourist information office on the railway station.

'Parlez-vous anglais?' I ask the pretty young lady behind the counter.

'Yes I do sir,' she replies confidently.

'Can you tell me how to get to this street please?' as I show her a piece of paper with the address written on it.

'You are here and you need to get to here,' she says as she circles both the station and the street on a map.

'How long will it take to walk?'

'About 15 minutes or three stops on the tram.'

'I'll walk; thank you so much for your help.'

Much heartened I follow the directions and within twenty minutes I find the road I am looking for. I follow it to the end and find Granny's Salon de Thé where everyone else has already arrived. Junior has a look of disbelief and happiness on his face. The worry lines disappear as I speak to him.

'I've made it,' I say proudly. 'Have you been here long?'

'Ten minutes or so,' he replies. 'We've just ordered something to eat so your timing is perfect.'

I ask for a croque madame, whereas the others have ordered croque monsieur.

'What's the difference?' asks Junior.

'Croque madame is the same as a croque monsieur with the addition of an egg on top. That is the only difference. I bet you're surprised to see me because you look it.'

'Yes and no; your navigation is not the best now is it?'

'Granted, and I do make more errors than most, but I get there eventually. All you ever do, and the others do as well, is just keep on about the mistakes; never do

I get any credit for the things I get right. And it happens more often than you think.'

'Well you're here now and that's all that matters.'

I didn't dare tell him about not knowing which stop to get off at or going into the tourist information office to ask for directions. Some things are best left unsaid. Plan 'B' has got off to a good start.

After we have eaten we make our way to the apartment. It is no more than 100 yards away from Granny's down a narrow side street in the old part of Nice. We make our way up two flights of stairs and I discover that the others have already checked in with the owner and have allocated the rooms. Cinders, PJ and Duracell have the ensuite room, Princess and Junior have the 'love nest' while Nettie and I have a spacious double room. We have a shared bathroom, which has everything we need. So far it all looks good.

After we have settled in we have a quick change of clothes and head for the beach, which is only two streets away. The sun is hot, there is very little breeze and so while everyone goes in the water I stay on the beach to do precisely nothing. It doesn't quite work out like that because the beach is entirely made up of large pebbles, the like of which we paid a small fortune for to go in our herb garden at home! I reckon there must be a point at which it would have been cheaper to bring a lorry down here and load up with stones rather than pay the fortune we did at home for the same thing.

Trying to get comfortable is not easy and after much experimenting I opt for laying flat on my back and trying not to move too much. I suppose it must be a similar technique to laying on a bed of nails, not that I've tried it …… yet! The stones are warm and with my hat over my face I do allow myself a little snooze; no I don't, I fall asleep, only to be woken up by a dripping wet Duracell who stands too close to me and makes me wet. We call her Duracell because, like the battery, she just seems to go on forever, long after her older sister is worn out.

'Grumpy, I don't like the stones because they hurt my feet,' she wails.

I was just about to console her when she changes the subject and momentarily forgets about her feet.

'Look Grumpy, a plane.'

'So it is and if you look carefully it is coming in to land over there where we did earlier today.'

'Is that the aeroplane station?' she asks innocently.

I want to laugh but don't because if you don't know the word then describing it with words that you do know shows an astute brain I reckon.

'The aeroplane station is called an airport. It's where planes take off and land,' I say.

'Air……?'

'Air….port. What is an aeroplane station called?'

'Airport Grumpy.'

'Well done.'

I ask her several more times during the coming days and she always answers correctly. The word has registered in her mind and is an addition to her growing vocabulary.

Flashes of lightening light up the sky and we feel the first drops of what proves to be a short sharp shower. However it is enough of a prompt to get us off the beach and back to the apartment. We don't stay there too long as the rain stops, so we go exploring. We head round the headland to the harbour and find out that the first port facilities date back to the mid 18th century. They were later extended several times in the late 19th and early 20th centuries.

While we are looking at the various pleasure craft young Duracell comes out with another wonderful observation while looking at the Corsican ferry.

'If you cut the strings the boat can swim,' she says.

It is wonderful logic from one so young. I'm sure the captain of the Corsican ferry will be delighted to know that his vessel 'can swim'!

19-07-13

After our long day yesterday, today starts very slowly. In drips and drabs we slowly surface, breakfast on baguette, ham and cheese and then as we realise that we really are in France, decisions start to get made, the first of which involves PJ and Duracell. They are getting restless and so Nettie and I, being the good grandparents that we are, take them to the beach and wait for everyone else to join us. One by one they turn up and it is as if PJ and Duracell have new playmates. I am gradually becoming surplus to requirements and so I whisper into Junior's ear as soon as he arrives, 'I'm going exploring. I'll catch up with you later.'

'Without a map?'

'Without a map,' I say. 'Don't look like that; I won't be more than a couple of hours.'

He looks worried even though he tries hard not to!

For my first bit of exploring I climb the steps to Fort Alban that overlooks the harbour and sits upon the headland over 200 metres above sea level. There are information boards detailing the history. It was built by the Duke of Savoy in order to defend Nice and nearby Villefranche. Construction began in 1557. The views from here are magnificent and after yesterdays rain the air is clear and so it proves a good photo opportunity as the heat haze is absent but I feel sure that it will return later in the day. It does.

I walk around the edge of an archaeological dig that is going on to uncover the remains of the cathedral dedicated to the Virgin Mary. Again, there are plenty of information boards to inform the discerning reader. It was built in the 11th and 12th centuries and then rebuilt in the late Middle Ages. With modern technology there is now a picture on display of a virtual rebuild of how it probably once looked. From there I walk to the highest point possible only to find a souvenir shop and I buy my postcards that I always send whenever I am away.

Not far away and a little lower down is a superb playground for children surrounded by trees and bushes to provide shade for all those playing on the apparatus and for those adults watching, as I will probably do later in the week.

Having seen all that I want to see I descend the mound, staying in the shade as best I can because the sun is raising the temperature by the minute. I make my way to Place Garibaldi and from there try to orientate myself with my arrival yesterday, studying bus routes and the tramline. The tram is a bonus because the bus tickets and tram tickets are interchangeable, as both are run by the same company. Validating a ticket on the bus is a requirement and I never saw anyone not do it. The fine, if caught is a minimum of €48.

Without consciously doing so I find myself almost back at the railway station so this time I do take the tram and then wander through some more narrow streets before arriving at the Cathedral Saint Reparate. I go inside because I am hot and I know that it will be cool in there. I am not wrong. I often go into places of worship just to have a look around and also for a bit of quiet contemplation.

From there I make my way back to the apartment only to be intercepted by Junior.

'Where have you been?' he asks me.

'To the fort and then wandered around the old town to get my bearings. Where have you been? You haven't been looking for me have you just because I've taken more than a couple of hours? I'm as fluid as anyone else when it comes to time you know.'

'No you're not, you are very precise about time that's why we get worried about you when you're over time.'

'Junior, you care about me, how sweet! Now where have you been since I can see that you have escaped the beach babes?'

'I went to the fort as well.'

'Were you following me?' I ask him accusingly.

Just then the beach babes join us and Princess makes an announcement. 'We're taking the girls to the fort on the train this afternoon, you know, the one that runs along the seafront. Anyone coming with us?'

'We've done it,' say Junior and I together.

'Oh, so you won't be coming then,' says Princess sounding disappointed.

'It's worth a look,' I say by way of encouragement. 'And I'll do it again, so I'll see you up there, but I'm going to walk.'

'I'm running,' says Junior boldly. 'I'll give Grumpy twenty minutes head start and meet him in the café area.'

'We're still going by train,' insists Princess.

After a bite to eat back at the apartment Princess, Cinders, Nettie and the two little ones make their way to the seafront to catch the train. I leave at the same time and start to walk. Junior reminds me that he has given me twenty minutes head start so decides to read his book to pass the time.

Within ten minutes I am in the café area and wait. Fifteen minutes later a breathless Junior looks hugely disappointed that I have beaten him to it but is gracious enough to accept defeat. He has been quicker than me covering the distance but twenty minutes was too big a handicap to overcome.

'Did you take the lift?' he asks accusingly.

'No I didn't.'

'Never mind tell me later how you did it.'

'I'll tell you now. I took the steps and that's all I did, honestly.'

His look told me that he wasn't convinced.

'Come on,' he says, 'let's go up, to the souvenir shop and meet the train.'

So we do. We arrive just before it did and are pleased to see everyone. Duracell and PJ are excited by their new adventure and want to run around and look at everything. They launch themselves at walls to try and see over them and how far down the drop goes. PJ is a little apprehensive at some of the drops and I feel that she is inheriting some of her mother's fear of heights. Duracell on the other hand has no such inhibitions. Junior and I keep an eye on her and stop her doing anything too daft just for her mother's sanity as much as anything else.

For the return trip the passengers return as they came, on the train.

Junior declares, 'I'm going to run behind the train.'

'Good luck to you in this heat. I'm going to walk. I'll meet you at the finish,' I say.

Off goes the train with Junior running behind it and me walking. The train has to take a long spiral route whereas I can take the more direct route of the steps. I am on the seafront long before the train. I am in a world of my own watching the joggers go by and wondering why anyone would want to jog on a hot day like today. Then one of them creeps up behind me and taps me on the shoulder. It's Junior. He passes me on my left side and points to the train just in front on my right side. I can see the end point a little further along on the Promenade des Anglais and realise that I will not be the first there.

'Run Forest run,' yells an encouraging Australian from on the train and aimed at Junior.

By the time the train stops I can see that Junior had kept up with it but now has his hands on his knees and is breathing heavily. A minute later I, too, have reached the end of the train line. Junior, despite his heavy breathing has a smile a mile wide on his face as he is basking in the glory of a round of applause from the people on the train.

We make our way slowly back to the apartment with a view to having a short rest and then getting changed to go out for the evening. If only it could be that simple! I make the most of the time writing three postcards, popping out to post them and then take my turn in the shower. While adjusting the nozzle the fixing falls off the wall, not that it was attached too well in the first place. I can see what needs doing and just require a screwdriver to make the repair. We don't have one between us so I use a kitchen knife and fortunately it works well enough to get the fixing back in place. I then adjust the height so that even the tallest has no need to touch it and then adjust the rose so that the water comes down more directly to wash the person under the shower and not the floor because the shower curtain is too short. Apart from that it is all perfect, and fingers crossed, my creative DIY will hold together for the rest of the holiday!

When we are all ready Nettie decides that she will baby sit, leaving the rest of us to take a stroll in the warm evening air, have an ice cream and then people watch from a nearby café. We sit at an outside table and watch the world go by. Late into the evening there are still plenty of people walking around so we decide to count how many different languages we can hear. The local rosé wine is chilled to perfection but with Junior dispensing the liquid by the thimbleful a bottle lasts a long time.

Into view comes a middle-aged woman walking her dog across the square. Then about ten metres from our table this little black dog suddenly stops and squats down. The owner yanks on the lead but the dog only stutters a footstep before stopping again and unloads the rest of what it had stopped to do in the first place. Thinking that as a responsible dog owner she might clear up the mess, she does nothing of the sort and carries on walking. Come to think of it I don't recall seeing any dog litter bins anywhere.

We watch as people cross the square, looking at mobile phones and other must have electrical gadgets but not looking where they are going. All of us stare in disbelief at how close people are to stepping into the mess but oblivious of doing so. No more than five minutes later a tall, elegantly dressed young lady, wearing wedge shoes steps into the first small pile, carries on walking totally unaware of what she has done. There are several more very near misses and then another young lady, glued to her mobile phone and not paying attention to where she is going, treads in the bigger heap and slides. Only then does she avert her gaze from the phone to her predicament. Her footwear is minimal and it now has the whole of the underneath covered in what the dog had been so keen to get rid of earlier. Naturally enough the smell quickly spreads around the square, heads turn to see where it has come from and the young lady in question looks suitably embarrassed. There is no grass area to clean her shoe and in the end she shakes off what she can and continues on her way. She is no longer looking at her phone!

The smell doesn't go away so we use that as our excuse to return to the apartment. It doesn't take much to amuse us and schadenfreud is something I do not approve of; but in this instance, I cannot help feeling that she has, in part, been the architect of her own downfall.

20-07-13

The incident is still being talked about this morning; not exactly the best of subjects to accompany croissants and coffee but it doesn't put anyone one off eating.

'Cinders and I are taking the girls to Phoenix Park today. Anyone else care to join us?' asks Nettie.

'I will,' I say, 'and we can use the ten-journey ticket that I have to get there.'

'OK. Anyone else?'

'Princess and I are off to Monaco,' declares Junior.

That was quick I think, but don't say anything. Decisions reached so quickly and without debate. Will it last I wonder? But before I become too cynical we go our separate ways. We catch the bus to the park, which is almost opposite the airport and then have a bit of a walk to the entrance.

'Can I go on your shoulders Grumpy? My legs are tired,' wails Duracell.

Soft as I am I give in to her pitiful cries even though I know that she will be fully charged and raring to go as soon as she sees the attractions. We arrive at the entrance and pay €2 per adult and the children go in free. Apart from the local buses it is the best value for money so far. Even the entrance tickets are beautifully printed and are worthy of keeping as a souvenir instead of being instantly discarded like so many tickets are.

As soon as we get through the barriers my immediate thoughts are to sit in the shade, listen to the classical music and watch the 'dancing waters'. That thought doesn't last long as PJ and Duracell have other ideas about what we will all do. We walk a little way before they both stop and look at the guinea pigs in their imaginatively designed area. There are enough old artefacts in there to keep me transfixed while they look at the animals.

'That one's eating a tomato Grumpy,' says Duracell pointing it out. 'And look at those two Grumpy, they're playing piggy back!'

'So they are,' I reply, trying to stifle a giggle.

'Can I have a guinea pig Grumpy?'

Before I can answer, the attention span has gone and it is on to the next attraction. We do our best to slow them down but PJ and Duracell are having none of it. They scoot around looking at everything and see nothing. Eventually Cinders decides to take them off to the play area while Nettie and I can enjoy some rare time alone together. The cacti gardens are particularly eye catching and all the plants look very healthy. In between the plants, at strategic points, are some imaginative sculptures, as there are in other parts of the grounds, but with warning notices telling people not to touch, as the sculptures are fragile.

From the cacti gardens we enter what I can only describe as a mini version of the Eden Project complete with the steamy, tropical area and the dry desert area. We go to the tropical area first and marvel at the plants, which Nettie gloats over, wishing she could have the same at home. As I am looking into an area sealed off by glass, I make one of my classically wrong observations.

'Those crocodiles are plastic. The pose is all wrong,' I confidently inform my wife. No sooner have I said it than the 'plastic' crocodile moves. A withering look from my other half sends me into silent mode for a while as she becomes absorbed in the plant life. The silence is getting to me as much as the humidity so I say, 'I'm going to find Cinders, I'm sure she could do with a break so I'll offer to look after the children and she can have a look in here. I think she'll enjoy it.'

I walk on and look at the rest of the tropical area before taking a stroll around the desert area. Then I make my way to the play area and find Cinders sitting in the shade watching her offspring having the time of their lives trying out all the apparatus. We swap places and she makes it into the biosphere before Duracell spots me.

'Grumpy, I'm thirsty,' she says.

'Come with me,' I reply and am promptly joined by PJ. I take them to a water tap just outside the play area and show them how it works. It is dark green in colour with a brass handle on the top. I turn the handle in a circular motion and the water flows out of the tap. Then I cup my hands together, catch some water and drink it. They think it is a new game and spend ages turning the handle so that they can drink the water; far more water than if it had been from a bottle. No bad thing on a hot day. Duracell, in particular turns the handle for anyone and everyone who wants some water. By the time I manage to prise her away from the tap she is soaked through. What Cinders or, more worryingly for me, Nettie will say, I daren't think about, since for them, it has to be bottled water and not tap water. I've lost count of the number of times that I've told them that our water company at home is French owned so maybe they have upped their game and know what they are doing. Eventually we all meet up again by which time PJ is flagging but Duracell is living up to her name.

'You're soaked!' observes Cinders, stating the obvious.

'I was thirsty,' replies Duracell.

'You're supposed to drink it not wear it!'

'Shoulders Grumpy.'

'Not until you're dry,' I reply.

'Did you let them drink tap water?' asks Nettie in clipped tones through clenched teeth.

'Yes dear, I did. It's perfectly drinkable. Lots of people are doing it if you care to observe.'

There is no reply.

'Furthermore, explain this to me as you are an aficionado on bottled water. How is it that the water that has been in the ground for millions of years gets put into a bottle and then has to be drunk by a certain date? How do the water diviners or whoever is responsible for finding the stuff know which water source is near to its use by date? I mean, what are the telltale signs? Explain that to me if you can.'

'Have you got the bus ticket?' asks Nettie. 'It's time to go.'

Ignoring the question and changing the subject is always a bad sign. I might have overstepped the mark. I'll have to be on my best behaviour now as I'm sure retribution will be sought. I mustn't have any more plastic crocodile moments!

As we make our way back to the exit we walk past the 'dancing waters', which are performing so we stop, listen and look. It has a calming effect, especially in the shade, but for PJ and Duracell it revitalises them. They stand too near the waters and start to get wet all over again. It really is time to go. Today has been a day for the children and they have had a great time, as we all have.

We don't have to wait too long for a bus to come along. When it arrives, we hop on and make the journey back along the seafront to the stop nearest our apartment. The two little darlings sleep soundly as soon as they go to bed despite the noise from outside.

Princess and Junior return from Monaco and tell us of their day. I listen as Junior tells me of walking the Formula One racetrack. I'm not a fan of the sport but I hoped that I might have accompanied him at some stage during our stay here but it is not to be. I would like him to explain the circuit and all the finer points of it so that I can have a better insight into the sport but I can't be in two places at once and I did have a cracking good day with the grandchildren.

21-07-13

I don't know what I was thinking about during the night but my first recollections of consciousness in the morning, that moment just before the eyes open, I am aware of rubbing, almost caressing my left arm with my right hand. It feels like I am running my hand over the pimples of an old-fashioned table tennis bat. The movement disturbs Nettie who quickly solves the problem.

'Honey, you've been bitten.'

'Mozzies!' I exclaim, and then look, now that my eyes have opened, and see that it isn't just one bite but several. I must have been 'chef's choice' last night as not just one mozzy but a whole squadron of the little blighters had their fill of me. Judging by the size of the lumps it's a wonder they can still fly. On a positive note the bites don't itch so I decline all medication and just tough it out. Every time I get bitten I think back to a holiday in Borneo when a local guide told me that the reason we westerners get bitten and he doesn't is because we smell too sweet! I wondered then if it applies to mosquitoes in general or if it was peculiar to Borneo. Whatever the answer, it is too late now, I have been bitten and it shows.

Over breakfast nobody has any plans for doing anything straight away so the beach seems the likely option. With that in mind I say, 'I fancy getting the bus to Monaco today. Does anyone wish to join me?'

The silence is deafening so off I go. I walk along the coast road, around the headland that Fort Alban is built on, along two sides of the harbour and rejoin the coast road towards Monaco. I look at the timetable on a bus stop and as the stops are not too far apart, decide to keep walking until a bus comes along. Three stops along the road and I note that a bus is due, so I wait at that stop and hop on, validate my ticket and sit down. The scenery is magnificent and holds my gaze for most of the journey. There are plenty of boats zipping along and people swimming in the Med but I notice that there is a definite lack of sandy beaches. They are mostly stony like the one we are frequenting.

All too soon the bus arrives at Monaco and as this is the final destination for this particular bus and not just a stop along the way to Menton, I decide to see which part of the Principality it stops in. I don't have to wait long to find out. The stop is at the end of a row of shops, not little village shops but major city stores. Shopping is not something I enjoy as a hobby so I don't spend any time looking in them. I am more the know what I want, see it, buy it and go type. I make my way to the harbour all the while looking for the telltale signs where the F1 track is that Junior told me about. The red and white markings are an obvious sign but less obvious are the small metal covers on the pavements and kerbs where the crash barriers are put in place for race day.

The harbour has its usual display of expensive yachts and gas-guzzlers and further out there is a cruise liner moored up. I don't see a huge amount of people milling around so maybe they have all been absorbed by the population or else been bussed off somewhere.

Forty years ago the harbour had a 'wow' factor for me but now I think that the rest of the world is catching up so it is no longer as impressive. Certainly the prestige is still here but I just feel that the area is now over-rated, over-priced and past it's best. That feeling was not allayed when I am charged an eye watering €7.50 for a small bottle of water and a cappuccino.

Moving on, I start to go uphill again towards the Palace passing on the way the Fairmont Hotel that has a sign outside which reads, 'Fairmont Hairpin The World's Most Famous Bend'. I have seen it on television and watched the cars racing towards it and then tackle the next bend further on. What I didn't appreciate, and no television camera or photograph can show, is just how steep the road is. I'm sure it requires great skill to tackle it at the speed the racing drivers do but I'm still left with the unaltered opinion that the Monaco F1 race is not so much a race as a procession as the overtaking opportunities are very few and far between. I'm sure Junior doesn't agree with me but he's not here to give me a different take on matters.

Eventually I arrive at the Palace and am impressed by how clean it all looks. Outside there are sentries in their crisp, white uniforms keeping guard and admonishing anyone who ventures too close, as I see one lady do, in search of a close-up photograph of something that catches her eye. There are cannons with a neat pile of cannon balls in a pyramid shape beside each one of them. More for show than to fire in anger I suspect. The views over the walls are stunning. There are little sheltered harbours all full of boats that can be seen from this vantage point and it only serves to show why people built their defences on high ground. The enemy could be seen from miles away and so tactics could be worked out. That was of course before the invention of the aeroplane, which would now attack from above! On my way down from the Palace I pass a church and beside it another, older church, both looking spotlessly clean. The older one looks like it has been carved out of sand but it isn't of course. I take several pictures for no better reason than to show Junior and Princess to see if they found these little gems. I bet they didn't.

Having seen all that I wanted to see, I make my way to the bus stop where I get into conversation with a young couple of Spanish backpackers.

'Excuse, are you English please?' asks the male.

'I am,' I reply.

'Do you know which is for Nice the bus?'

'Yes; number 100.'

'Sank you. Do you catch it from where?'

'Here in five minutes.'

'Sank you.'

Having gained the information they wanted they start talking to each other in Spanish while studying a map. So engrossed are they that I have to interrupt them and point out that the bus is on its way. Either we all make it to Nice or we all get lost together I think to myself. Luckily I manage to get a seat on the bus again. It isn't always easy as the buses are well used.

When the bus arrives back in Nice I get off at the harbour and take a leisurely stroll back around the harbour, passing the impressive war memorial before stopping off at Granny's to have a pancake. The ever-knowledgeable waiter recognises me and says that everyone else is on the beach. I thought they would be but I don't fancy sitting on the warm stones, so I make the pancake last.

By evening time we have all re-assembled and Junior has a sad look about him.

'What's up?' I ask.

'It's my last night here. I've got to get back to work for an important meeting.'

'Can't you call in sick?'

'No I can't. The meeting is important and besides the flight is booked.'

'Fair enough; I'll see you off at the airport if Princess doesn't mind.'

'Fine by me,' she says.

'I thought that you might be glad of the company on the way back from the airport, that's all,' I add by way of an explanation.

'If you're sure; I hadn't thought about it.'

'I have and I'll introduce you to the delights of the shuttle bus between terminal one and terminal two and also the local bus 23 for getting back here.'

'Alright then,' she says sounding less than convinced.

Junior packs his bag and decides upon the venue for his 'Last Supper' with us. Sadly it proves a profound disappointment as we wait almost an hour to be served and when we are, half the food doesn't arrive. PJ and Duracell fall asleep at the table so we abandon the restaurant and go back to the apartment. It is not how Junior planned to spend the evening at all. Thereafter we give the place a wide berth for the rest of our stay.

22-07-13

It is another slow start today. It almost feels like waking up with a hangover, which it is of a sort. It isn't the alcohol-fuelled, self-inflicted variety but one caused by the disappointment of Junior's 'Last Supper'. Sensing that the sombre mood might make savage inroads into the morning I try to lighten things up by saying, 'I'm going exploring again, anybody going to join me?' I try to stay upbeat but all I get in reply is, 'We're probably going to the beach until we decide on something.'

'Fair enough,' I say and start to leave.

'Where are you going?' ask Junior.

'Exploring.'

'Where exactly?'

'I don't know where exactly because that is the fun of exploring; one never knows where it will lead to. See you when I get back.' This time I do leave and I don't even turn round to see if Junior has got his worried look on again! I know exactly where I am going and what I am going to do. I don't declare my hand because

I am searching for information and I need to have it all ready for tomorrow morning's inevitable conversation.

I make my way round the corner, find the tram stop, hop on the first tram that comes along and head for the tourist information centre at the railway station.

'Bonjour madam,' I say in my best French.

'Bonjour monsieur, how may I help you?' the good looking lady asks me, knowing straight away that I am English.

'Can you tell me which number bus I need to catch to go to Eze and where do I catch it from please?'

'You need bus 82 and you catch it from Le Port.'

'I know where that is,' I say proudly. 'Thank you so much for your help.'

'You are most welcome monsieur. Au revoir.'

With my task complete I catch the tram and make my way back, getting off three stops later and head for the beach. There I find everyone having a great time splashing about in the water in an upbeat mood far removed from the morose feeling of first thing. I'm not too enamoured by the green flecks sticking to their bodies as they leave the water but nobody is too concerned as it soon washes off under the beach shower. Duracell still has her own issues with the stones that make up the beach. I am just getting myself comfortable with my 'bed of nails' position on the stones when Junior appears.

'There you are,' he says pointing at me. 'You're hard to spot without your yellow hat on.'

'So it does have some uses then.'

'Of course it does. When you wander off as you do, at least we can see you at a distance when we need to find you. Taking it off throws us out a bit. We have to look harder.'

'Shall I put it back on then?'

'There's no need to. I've found you.'

'Well I'm going to. The temperature is at least 35°C again so I better had to protect my head and besides, with this design of hat I don't need to wear sunglasses. It's more than just a "spot Wally" item.'

'Ooooooh, a bit touchy aren't we?'

'Not at all. Just giving you an explanation. Besides, why the sour face? You look like you've been sucking a lemon.'

'Firstly, I'm going home this afternoon, which I don't want to do because I quite like it here and secondly I've got 84 emails from work to deal with.'

'How do you know?' I ask, curiosity getting the better of me.

'I've checked up on my lap top.'

'What? You're supposed to be on holiday and leave all that stuff behind.'

'Not these days you don't. Work never stops. I don't have to answer them until I'm back in the office but I need to be aware of what's going on.'

'So when do you get a proper break?'

'I don't, not like you had from the factory floor. These days it's all different.'

'It's not an improvement, that's for sure.'

'It's the way of the world now.'

'Not in my world it isn't. Anyway, that's enough talk about work. When are you leaving for the airport?'

'In a couple of hours. Fancy a beer?'

'Certainly do,' I reply and we both go off to slake our thirst and have a sandwich.

At the set hour Princess, looking as glamorous as ever, joins us and we make our way along the seafront to the Promenade des Anglais in order to catch a bus directly to terminal two. At the airport I make myself scarce while Princess and Junior share some tender moments together before he makes his way through security and eventually to board the plane back home.

Princess and I catch the shuttle bus back to terminal one where I buy another €10 ticket for another ten journeys. I then introduce her to the delights of bus 23 and this time I pay attention to where I am going so that I will know which stop to get off at. Both of us, at the same time, agree the stop and we get off. It is then that I realise where I went wrong on my first day. I don't tell Princess and on reflection; staying on the bus for longer than I needed to on the first day and finding the tourist information office was a bonus.

When we return to the apartment PJ says to me, 'Grumpy, can we see the plane take off please?'

'Of course we can. If we go now we can stand on the seafront and watch it.'

'How will we know which one it is Grumpy?'

'It will have an orange tail, just like the plane we flew in on.'

By the time we reach the seafront, planes are taking off at regular intervals. We don't have to wait long.

'There it is Grumpy,' says PJ pointing to the sky. 'Is he on that one?'

I look at my watch. The time is right so quite possibly he is.

'Let us wait a few more minutes and see if there are any other orange tails,' I suggest.

We wait but don't see any.

'No more Grumpy; that was his plane. Do you think he saw me waving?'

'I'm sure he did if he was sitting on the left side of the plane.'

'I'll ask him if he saw me when we get home. I'm going to miss him Grumpy.'

'We all will PJ but just think, in two days time we'll see him again when we get home.'

As days go this was a quiet one, but for me a useful one in as much as I have my next adventure sorted out should I need to resort to Plan 'B' again.

23-08-13

Just moving around in bed at an early hour brings me out in a sweat. I'm sure it's hotter than ever today. Not having air-conditioning in the apartment doesn't help but nobody is complaining. We are all up and about before eight o'clock and it is Princess who speaks first about her intentions for the day.

'I'm off to Monaco with PJ, Duracell and Cinders. We are going in the swimming pool. Anyone else going to join us?'

'I will,' says Nettie.

'How about you Grumpy?' asks Princess.

'I went yesterday; why didn't you come with me then?'

'We were on the beach and in the sea swimming,' chips in Nettie.

'And now you are going to do the same in Monaco.'

'Yes,' she replies.

'Enjoy yourselves, have fun.'

'Where are you going?'

'Eze, by bus.'

'Princess wants to go there,' says Nettie.

'She still can; she can come with me.'

'But we're going to Monaco.'

'And I'm going to Eze; right now,' and start to leave. I can see that this is going to turn into one of those pointless going-round-in-circles conversations that I desperately try to avoid.

'Do you know how to get there?' asks Nettie, now getting concerned for me being on my own again and without Junior to worry about me.

'Yes I do. I did my research yesterday.'

'Oh? Well have a good day.'

'You too,' and then I do leave.

As I make my way to the seafront, then around the headland, and two sides of the harbour I replay the conversation over and over again in my head. I decide that all things are possible with a little bit of thought and planning but whenever I mention it I am shot down in flames with ridiculous phrases like 'we're on holiday' or 'that's what life is all about' and best of all 'you just want to rush around at breakneck speed like you're on a mission,' and that just isn't true. I like to get the most out of my time on holiday and not waste it dithering or having conversations that go nowhere. Hence Plan 'B'.

Eventually I arrive at the area of the bus stops and have to go searching for the correct one for Eze. Fortunately each stop has the numbers of all the buses that leave from it and the relevant timetables pinned up. I find the one I am looking for and have to wait a while because the buses are not that frequent. When bus 82 comes along I get on, validate my ticket and manage to get a seat. Within a few minutes the bus pulls away and heads inland up a winding mountain road to the village eleven kilometres away. Eze dates back to medieval times. The village itself is built around the base of a rock, upon which a castle sits. Locally it's known as the Eagle's nest and is 427metres above sea level. The views are even more spectacular than on the road to Monaco. The last part of the road into the village goes over a spectacular viaduct, which is beautiful in it's own right.

Unfortunately, my first impression of the village is that of a tourist trap enhanced by several coaches in the car park adjacent to the road so I decide to stay on the bus and go to the end of the route. It is only another four stops further on. The bus stop is Plateau de la Justice; each bus stop is named. I get off and read the timetable so that I can plan my day accordingly. I walk further up the road to the apex and see where it winds down the other side of the mountain. Around me are signs indicating woodland walks but with no map I don't think it wise to chance my luck. The panoramic views continue to keep me in a state of awe and on my return to the bus stop I take several pictures that I'd earmarked earlier.

Thirst is getting the better of me, so I call into a café adjoining a hotel and ask for an orange juice. The man who comes out from a back room to serve me at the bar is dressed in just a pair of shorts and flip-flops. With his bare top and droopy moustache he could just as easily have stepped out of a spaghetti western. Appearances can be deceptive though, as he is polite and courteous but short on conversation. After serving me he returns to the back room to continue watching the television set that I had taken him away from.

Any thoughts that I had of it being cooler in the mountains are ill founded, as there isn't any noticeable difference between here and the coast. I finish my ice-cold drink and walk back to Eze, stopping regularly to take pictures and to enjoy the views. The road is separated from the pavement by gardens with alternate trees displaying red and pink flowers. Below them and in between are lavender bushes, amongst other colourful flowers, all in full bloom. The whole scene looks just too pretty to be on the side of a road. I could name many people who would love their gardens to look as good as this!

When I eventually get back to the village, I climb up the rock as far as I can. I look down on a hotel garden of cacti and close to it a giant chessboard. I continue on and negotiate a labyrinth of narrow streets containing restaurants and souvenir shops at every twist and turn. No corner is left untouched. Eventually I reach a vantage point and the views are the best so far. Looking down on the powerboats and the wash they create seems the same as looking up to the sky and seeing a plane's vapour trails. It is quite some view.

On the descent through the claustrophobic alleyways I come out at a different place to the one I entered. It doesn't matter, as I am glad to be out of the confined space. I look up and see a signpost indicating Monaco 6.5 kilometres, about 4 miles. Under normal circumstances that is a distance I can easily walk and start to do so. I have only gone two or three paces when I hear a voice in my head telling me not to do it. The voice of reason points out that the temperature is 38° C and that I have no water bottle with me. I am not equipped to do the walk. I try to ignore the voice and take two more steps before the voice repeats the warning in a louder voice. I take heed this time and return to the village.

Part of me is disappointed that I won't be able to surprise everyone in Monaco and part of me is pleased to be able to explore a bit more of Eze. The town doesn't offer up any more little gems but the viaduct is certainly worth a look. It was built between 1911 and 1914 to complete an inner coastal road. It spans 80 metres over the Gaffinel Ravine and is called the Bridge of the Devil. I am curious as to why it should be so named. I find a shop that isn't too busy and chance my luck by asking the shopkeeper how the bridge got its name. He seems surprised at my question but tells me in very good English that local legend has it that a deal was struck between an old peasant, who hated losing time crossing the ravine to get to his fields each day, and the devil. The deal was a bridge in exchange for the soul of the first living creature to cross it. The peasant slept badly with a troubled conscience and it was made no better when, in the morning the bridge had been constructed and the devil was waiting on the other side. The peasant threw a stick onto the bridge and his dog chased after it thereby offering his soul to the devil. Satan was not happy at being fooled and it is said that he is still waiting.

'You have been warned,' said the kindly shopkeeper with a twinkle in his eye.

'Merci monsieur,' I say and leave the shop still unsure as to whether he had a laugh at my expense or not.

After walking over the viaduct a couple of times I look at the queue waiting for the bus and decide to walk back to the Plateau de la Justice bus stop. My thoughts are that there won't be too many people catching the bus from there so I will be certain of getting a seat. Walking up the hill is an effort and I stop frequently as the heat of the day has not lessened one bit and is getting to me. If ever I needed proof that the walk to Monaco was not a good idea, badly equipped as I am, then this is it. By the time I reach the last but one stop I have had enough. I sit on the seat in the open fronted shelter and wait, quite contentedly, for the bus. I have plenty of time to wait but it doesn't bother me, as I'm glad to sit down.

Five minutes before the bus arrives I am joined by a young lady who is in a world of her own listening to her ipod. We get on the bus and have our pick of the seats. When the bus gets into Eze the waiting crowd swarms on and it is standing room only as the bus pulls away. My instincts have proved me right. The descent is skilfully negotiated by the driver who, no matter how many times he or she does it, can never have less than 100% concentration as it is all twists and turns made even harder when meeting oncoming traffic.

We arrive safely back in Nice and I get off at Le Port. I amble back slowly to the apartment to await the others and compare notes. Along the way I am passed by the fitness fanatics of both genders jogging with their ipods in, some so loud that I can hear the hissing of the sound tracks. Sweat glistening on bronzed bodies, some so beautiful that I turn and take a second look!

I haven't been back long before I hear the patter of tiny feet on the stairs and Duracell hammering on the door. I let her in and she soon starts telling me of her day in the Principality. While she is doing so PJ comes in and looks shattered, closely followed by Princess, Cinders and Nettie. Try as they might they still haven't worn her out yet. She is living up to her name!

'Did you take many pictures Grumpy?' asks Princess.

"Yes I did; would you like to see them?'

'Later.'

She doesn't and I don't pursue the matter as Princess, the matriarch-in-waiting, drops a bombshell; 'We have all eaten, except Nettie, and we think that it will be a good idea if just the two of you ate out, alone, together.'

I am about to speak when a finger is put across my lips indicating me to stay silent. I need no further prompting. We both get changed in record time and walk to the square. The place is packed but we find a table for two near the fountain and order a meal. The chilled rosé wine is the first thing to be served and we are half way through it before the meal, a simple pizza, arrives. It may only be a pizza but they are as good as any from neighbouring Italy and vastly superior to those we get at home.

Our idyll is constantly interrupted by people crowding nearby posing for pictures close to the fountain. Inevitably our table is bumped into and although most apologise, it does get a bit tiresome. By the time we are half way through the second bottle of wine I'm past caring about the inconvenience and start to cast an eye over the perpetrators. Realisation rears its head when a swift kick on the shins reminds me that I am being spoken to and haven't replied. It is time to pay up and go.

We take a slow walk back and quietly enter the apartment, hoping not to disturb anyone only to find that PJ and Duracell have fallen asleep in our bed. Cinders is asleep in her en-suite room all alone, Princess is alone in hers and pining for Junior or is that snoring we can hear? Which just leaves us the problem of where we are going to sleep. Any thoughts of a nightcap and a cosy end to the day are long gone.

24-07-13

As I slowly wake up to yet another hot morning I realise that a week has passed. Where has the time gone? I wonder. Before packing there is the small matter of mending the fridge door. It isn't the fridge itself that is the problem but the flat-pack door that someone has attached to the fridge door that has parted company with the door it was supposed to be attached to. As we have no screwdrivers with us and as I managed to fix the shower with a kitchen knife I am tasked with fixing this problem.

First of all I have to undo six screws from the fixings on the side of the fridge door itself. The screws are of the crosshead variety and whereas a kitchen knife solved the earlier problem it doesn't solve this one. With another inspired piece of creativity I try a potato peeler and this does indeed work. After undoing all six screws I reassemble the sliding mechanism, put the screws back in place and tighten them up. I try the door a couple of times and everything works fine. We all agree not to use the fridge again. Looking around the place it appears that a few of the other fixings are not as good as they should be, including the screws to the front door lock!

The next task is to clean the apartment before the final inspection and the handing back of the key. This is where Cinders excels. She is the best there is when it comes to cleaning. As she rallies the troops I am called to attention.

'Grumpy, will you take PJ and Duracell to the park while we get cleaned up here please?'

'Certainly,' I reply. This way it gets me out of my least favourite job and one I've been told in the past that I'm not very good at anyway. My case is packed and I am ready for departure, the grandchildren are the same so the three of us walk to the park for playtime.

'I can't walk that far,' wails PJ.

'Shoulders Grumpy,' says a wide-eyed pleading Duracell.

'You will both walk. It isn't far and we will use the lift so that neither of you will have to walk up the steps,' I tell them taking a hard line on matters.

Neither argues and they both walk quite agreeably, having failed to get one over on me. Within ten minutes we arrive at the foot of the rock and head for the tunnel, which leads to the lift. There is no queue so we get in. Moments later we are 90 metres higher up as we step out of the lift and come face to face with an iron railing separating us from a vertical drop to oblivion. The girls gasp at the sight and I quickly usher them round the small concrete pathway and point them in the direction of the park.

PJ opens the gate and systematically tries every piece of apparatus. Duracell takes her time, weighing it all up and then follows on, but in her own way. She doesn't trail after her older sister. Also it is fascinating to see them inter-acting with children of other nationalities when they don't share a common language. One way or another they do communicate and have a great time.

Duracell then starts to run from one piece of apparatus to another and it isn't long before PJ follows her because she thinks that her little sister is having more fun. Duracell then spots a cargo net pyramid, towering about five metres to the apex. She goes off to explore it. I don't think she will get too far with it as the distance between the ropes is too great for her little legs. Meanwhile PJ is doing another round of the apparatus. To keep watch on both of them I need Marty Feldman eyes. Eventually my task is made easier when PJ decides to join her little sister. Thinking that she will get one over on her, PJ starts to climb the ropes and gets as far as the first disc, about one third of the way up the centre pole. At this point Duracell is still weighing up the options. PJ thinks about going higher but decides against it as the height is troubling her so she climbs down and returns to the roundabout. Little sister is like a rat up a drainpipe and scampers up to the first disc in no time at all. It certainly surprises me as she uses all of her arm strength and agility to make a nonsense of my prediction. She stops briefly, then eyes the second disc two thirds of the way up the pole and quickly makes it to that level. Now I am getting concerned as she eyes the apex but of equal concern is how she will get down. As I am thinking it she swings down from rope to rope with lightening speed, looks across at me with an expression that says. 'You didn't think I could do that did you Grumpy?'

While I am coming to terms with it all she runs off to join PJ for another circuit of the apparatus. I look at my watch and am surprised to see that we have been here for two hours. I call them over.

'It's time to go girls. Have you had a good time?'

'Yes Grumpy,' they both say.

We make our way down to street level and start walking back to Granny's where I have arranged to meet everyone else.

'Shoulders Grumpy,' pleads Duracell and this time I give into her much to the annoyance of PJ.

'Why does she always get a lift and not me?'

'Because I can only carry one on my shoulders and you are twice her age,' I reply.

'Not fair.'

PJ sulks and stomps all the way back. We are the first to arrive and so I treat the girls to a drink of fruit juice, which puts me back in favour again. We haven't been here too long when Cinders and her band of cleaners join us. They look like Cinders has had them grafting and are pleased to be away from the job. Cinders is smiling so I guess it's a job well done. We all have one last drink, say our goodbyes to the waiter, who has been attentive to our needs all week and leave. As a parting gift he gives PJ a toy aeroplane as she has been playing with it most of the week. I didn't even have time for a last look in the apartment. My case has been brought down for me and as I travel on hand luggage only, moving it is no hardship.

We keep in the shade as much as possible and make our way along the seafront to the Promenade des Anglais to catch the local bus to Phoenix Park where we will spend the afternoon before walking the short distance to the airport. I have a chuckle to myself when everyone now talks quite matter-of-factly about using the local buses and the ten-journey ticket when a week ago it was deemed too complicated! With money running low it is just as well that I had the foresight to explore this method of transport.

We pay our €2 to enter the park and once inside the usual first line is uttered by someone.

'What are we going to do? We need to put these cases somewhere.'

'We are going over there to the shaded area where I am going to spend the afternoon minding the cases and listen to classical music while you may do whatever you wish without the worry of trailing your cases around,' I say firmly.

'Really Grumpy, you don't mind?' says Cinders.

'Not at all, go and enjoy it all. I had all the excitement I needed this morning.'

'If you're sure.'

'I'm sure.'

Just as they all depart, leaving me alone in the shade, the music starts. The fountains spray water in rhythmic patterns and it is the most tranquil of settings. I am overdressed anyway so staying in the cool suits me fine. Besides that, I enjoy classical music. During the next few hours I am checked up on at regular intervals to make sure that I really am content to sit with the cases. To each and everyone I assure them that I am.

Eventually it is time to go. Duracell is now starting to show signs of tiredness. It has only taken a week! We gather our cases and make our way via an underpass to the airport and terminal one. Here we board the shuttle bus for terminal two. Melancholy is setting in.

Cinders makes sure that the worst of the dirt is off the children by cleaning them up in the airport washroom so that they will be ready for bed when they get home.

'Did everyone enjoy the holiday?' I ask as we make our way through security.

'We did,' they all say at once.

'How about you Grumpy? Did you enjoy it?' asks Cinders.

'I certainly did.'

'Was there anything else that you would like to have done but didn't get time to do?'

'I always have more to do than I can actually get done so if I was here for longer I would get the bus to Cannes for a day or two and then maybe a bus to Menton.'

'Why Menton?'

'To have a look around and then walk over the border to Italy, just because…..'

'So you'd come back here again?'

'I wouldn't rule it out, but then again I say that about almost everywhere I've been. I just enjoy travelling. For me the journey is as important as the destination, even if it's a local bus ride, like here.'

'There's no stopping you is there Grumpy?'

'No Cinders, there isn't and long may it continue. This whole week has been great fun, especially with so many of us together. The children have been good. Did I tell you what they got up to when I took them to the park this morning? Did I tell you how high Duracell climbed up the rope pyramid?'

'Stop right there; you know what I'm like with heights.'

'If you could have seen her,' I tease.

'I don't want to know.'

I smile, Cinders laughs and the pilot waves at the children as we board the plane. I sit beside Nettie of whom I have not seen enough of this past week and say to her, 'We ought to do this again sometime.'

She smiles and says, 'Let's get home from this one first before you start planning again. I know what you're like.'

We arrive home in the early hours of the morning. There on the doormat is a letter addressed to me. I open it and read what it has to say.

'Mmm, that sounds interesting,' I say in a voice louder than I intend.

'What's interesting?' replies Nettie.

'Nothing dear,' I lie; but in my head plans are being made.

Krakow

09-09-13

'Why Krakow?' asks Nettie. 'There are plenty of other places in the world.'

'I know there are, but I've wanted to go there for a long time and now an opportunity has arisen.'

'So who is this Lady F then?'

'The lady who wrote the letter that was here when we got back from Nice.'

'And?'

'And she would like me to go to Krakow with her to meet someone who is researching his family history. She has tracked down some documents here for him and is going to deliver them by hand.'

'You do come out with some strange things at times but this is the best yet. If you want to go, just go.'

'You are invited as well,' I say as an after thought.

'I'm not going to Poland, no way, but if you want to go, I won't stop you,' came the frosty reply.

'Thank you gorgeous; oh by the way we are making an early start in the morning so I'm staying at hers tonight, if that's alright with you. We are going out for a meal, goat curry actually, you can drop me off if you like and join us for the meal.'

'Don't push it! Goat curry? Is there such a thing? You do come out with some absurd things at times. Just go.'

'Thank you sweetheart,' I say in my best trying to be sincere voice.

Before the conversation gets any further Junior turns up and Nettie tells him what I'm up to.'

'Poland!' he says, almost spitting the word out. 'It's empty; they're all over here.'

'No they're not. You're just bigoted.' I tell him.

'If you get lost, how will you be able to ask for directions? You don't even speak Polish!'

'I know I don't; could be fun though couldn't it?'

Junior's face paled and I swear I can see another couple of worry lines etching their way across his brow.

'I'll send you a text every day just to let you know how I'm getting on. Alright?' I say trying to put his mind at rest.

'Who is Lady F?' he asks.

'Your mother will explain. Must go, I've got a bus to catch.'

Junior has a startled look about him. He turns to his mother for an explanation.

'He isn't going to Poland by bus; he's getting a bus to Colchester, staying overnight then getting a coach to

Stansted for an early flight to Krakow. Don't look so worried. He'll be fine.'

Junior doesn't look convinced. That is the last I will see of them for a few days as I finally leave for the railway station, which is where the bus departs from.

It is on time and I meet up with Lady F in Colchester as arranged, walk back to her flat and dump my case before heading to the pub for our meal. We are perusing the menu when the barman approaches. 'Can I help you?' he asks.

We have a table booked and are just wondering what to have off the menu?' replies Lady F.

'It's not a choice; that is the meal.'

'All of it!' I ask.

'All of it,' he repeats.

We are shown through to the dining area, take our seats and enjoy an excellent meal served by attentive waitresses. The goat curry was the main dish of a three-course meal.

'So what did you tell your wife?' Lady F asks me.

'I said that I was going to Krakow with you to deliver some papers to a friend of yours to help with his family history research.'

'And she believed you?'

'Probably not but I did ask her to join us so that you could explain it all to her. I mentioned that we were dining out on goat curry at which point she nearly threw up and sent me on my way. I said that I was travelling with Lady F, and was just getting around to explaining who you are when Junior turned up.'

'That's outrageous! I'm not a titled lady am I?'

'No but you are female and your initial is "F" so I just put the two together in one of my mad moments.'

'How did Junior take it?'

'I wasn't going to tell him but he called round unexpectedly so I had no choice since I was standing at the door ready to leave with suitcase in hand. He wasn't happy about me going away, so to pacify him I promised to send him a text every day. I've done it before and it seems to solve the problem. He does admit to enjoying them because he looks forward to the end of a working day and having something to read. He doesn't have his phone on during working hours.'

We finish our meal and make our way back to the flat for an early night before the journey begins.

Text to Junior: ***Arrived Colchester. Dined out on goat curry.***

10-09-13

It is twilight as we make our way on foot to the bus station in order to catch the coach to Stansted airport. With only two pick ups along the way the journey soon passes but not without incident. Between stops there is a loud crack as a stone hits the windscreen. Fortunately it doesn't shatter and neither is it in the sight line of the driver. We arrive at the airport, disembark and head for the terminal building, while the other passengers change coaches for their onward journey to Heathrow airport. The damaged coach then returns to Ipswich, where it started out from, for repairs.

Lady F and I clear security without incident, have a coffee then board the plane where I promptly fall asleep for an hour. During that time, so I am told afterwards, drinks were served over me to the other passengers in my row. We touch down and are told over the intercom that 'this is another on time flight'. I look out of the window and airports being airports I could be anywhere in the world.

As we disembark and clear passport control Lady F turns to me and says. 'We will be picked up here by my man in Poland. Speak of the devil, there he is waving at us.'

'So who is he exactly?'

'The person who emailed me and said that he thought that his family and mine are related.'

'And are they?'

'Probably, but you are more clued up on how it works than I am and knowing that you had a desire to come to Poland, at some point, to visit Auschwitz I thought now would be a good opportunity for you to do it. Carpe Diem and all that!'

'Visit Auschwitz?'

'Yes and also help with the family history. Kill two birds with one stone.'

Lady F introduces me to Cooper, her man in Poland, a slim, well spoken young man, in his late twenties, who speaks perfect English. He suggests that we have a coffee and get to know each other, which we do. The conversation goes so well that he is kind enough to drop us off at our apartment and agrees that we shall meet up again on another evening when he will bring his heavily pregnant wife with him if she feels up to it.

'What a thoroughly pleasant young man,' I say to Lady F. 'How long have you known him?'

'Apart from a couple of email exchanges as long as you have.'

'And you were prepared to come to Poland, alone, and meet up with someone you have only exchanged emails with?'

'I wouldn't have come on my own but I knew you wouldn't take too much persuading so that's why I sent the letter and made the arrangements with Cooper.'

'So what's the family connection?'

'I'm not entirely sure but I think he wants to know how the baby will be related. He gets in a muddle, so he says, with cousins being once or twice removed. He doesn't know how it works and neither do I but I knew you did so you can explain it to him.'

'And you brought me all this way to tell him?'

'Not complaining are you?'

'Not at all; it's very simple really.'

'Well save it until we meet up again and explain it over dinner.'

The apartment is five minutes walk from the city centre on the fourth floor of an older building with two locks on the front door and three on the apartment door. Inside, the two bedrooms are huge. One has a double bed and could easily accommodate another two double beds; similarly the other bedroom has twin beds and could easily take another four single beds. The lounge has a settee that pulls out to make a double bed. The only disappointment is the bathroom, which is tiny. The shower is too small to bend down in but that apart all the facilities are new and modern. In the bedrooms the wooden wardrobes, tables and chairs are solid and old fashioned. It will suit us fine, as we are solid and old fashioned!

After a quick change of clothes we head off to explore the city. The first place that we go to is the modern shopping complex that combines the shops, bus station and railway station. It's an impressive set up. While we are here, we find out the best way to get to Auschwitz. We have a choice of an organised trip or to make our own way by either train or bus. We choose the bus; find out the departure times and where to purchase our tickets from in the morning. At this point I have a feeling of sadness creep over me, as I am sure that tomorrow will be a difficult day.

Next we take a look inside a couple of churches and Lady F lights a candle for relatives now passed. The city has a good feel to it. It is not over large and is easily walkable. Having not eaten since early this morning we feel it is time to satisfy the hunger pangs.

We dine handsomely on trout, fried potatoes and vegetables all washed down with a Polish lager and Polish vodka. I like to try the local drinks as well as the food, it would be rude not to! Lady F does not share my enthusiasm; she raises her eyebrows with an air of 'if you must'. We are part way through our meal when the lights dim, there is a fanfare of music and a dish like a giant donor kebab is ceremoniously brought to a nearby table, carried by a man in national costume. The 'meal on a stick' is passed through a naked flame a couple of times before being placed on a plate at the table. It has all the pomp and ceremony of the Scots piping in the haggis. The music stops, the lights come back on and everything returns to normal.

Text to Junior: ***Arrived Krakow. Have discovered vodka. All is well.***

11-09-13

We wake at 06-30. The blue of yesterday has given way to a grey, leaden sky this morning. The rain is a steady drizzle and looking out from the lounge window over the uninspiring roof tops, littered with satellite dishes, the bleakness of the scene looks as though it has been ordered, just for us, to set the scene for our trip to Auschwitz.

After a quick breakfast we hurry through the rain to the bus station, buy our tickets and board the bus to Oswiecim, which is 60 kilometres away. The bus is not much bigger than a minibus and we are full up before the journey starts. Along the way passengers continue to get onboard, meaning that by the time we reach our destination, those of us fortunate enough to have a seat, are just as squashed as those standing. One and a half hours later we are glad to get off and walk the short distance to the entrance. It is still drizzling, the sort of fine persistent drizzle that slowly soaks in rather than the steady rain that has one reaching for an umbrella straight away.

The first thing that we become aware of, and this does come as a surprise, is just how many coaches there are in the car park. We walk briskly to the ticket office, pay our money and are given a yellow sticker along with a headset and a radio receiver and told to wait. Just as we are wondering what the sticker is for we find out. A sign is hoisted with the word 'POLSKA' on it and all those people with red stickers fall into line. When the 'ENGLISH' sign goes up it is for all of us with yellow stickers. Our guide leads us outside, checks that we can all hear him through the headset and begins the tour.

'Good morning ladies and gentlemen, let us begin the tour at the main gate. You see that sign "ARBEIT MACHT FREI", do you know what it means? It means "WORK MEANS FREEDOM", another German lie! It is one of many lies they told.' It is the opening gambit from our guide; a tall well built Pole in his late twenties with close cut hair who speaks impeccable English, the result of having lived in England for two years. That sets the tone for his dialogue. There is no 'welcome to Auschwitz' or Hollywood sugar coating put on it, this is in your face, straightforward, unsavoury facts! He continues. 'That is not the original sign, that was stolen in 2009 and found two days later in the north of the country in three pieces, this is a replacement. Are you surprised to see brick buildings?'

We all mumble a collective 'Yes'

'That is because it was originally built for the Polish army. It was their barracks until the Germans took over. It was here that first of all the Polish political prisoners were housed and then later the Jews. The murders started here but they couldn't kill them fast enough so Auschwitz II was built. We will go there later. When the war turned against the Germans they tried to destroy everything but failed. Here we will see what remains.'

While we are listening to this we are walking between the barrack huts. The puddles forming on the unmetalled roadways are getting deeper as the drizzle continues. Already I notice an edge to the guide's delivery. He doesn't use the word 'kill' it is always 'murder', it isn't a 'prisoner of war camp' it is a 'death camp' As we make our way inside one of the buildings we see a sign that reads, **'Jews are a race that must be totally exterminated' Hans Frank 1944 Governer** (sic) **General in Nazi occupied Poland.** The rain continues and is adding to the misery we can both feel. We move from building to building and see, in turn, piles of human hair, two large heaps of footwear, two more large cases of prosthetics. There are hundreds of suitcases all marked with personal details. There are heaps of empty gas canisters that were used to gas the inmates. It is awful. There are black and white pictures that have been seen on television in various documentaries over the years but seeing them in person doesn't lessen the sadness, it makes it worse. Lady F is unusually quiet. No one speaks above a whisper; I am numb with the horror of it all. I wonder if I'll ever laugh again, smile again or even have a reason to be cheerful.

We move on and see the basic, primitive washrooms, toilets and the three tiered bunk beds. We see many photographs of the captured Jews in their striped clothing with personal details listed underneath. Back outside we are taken to the Death Wall where prisoners were shot. There are many candles burning and bunches of flowers placed in memory of those who were a victim here.

'Do you know how old the youngest person was to be shot here? Nine years old. Can you imagine shooting a nine year old child?' our guide asks us.

We don't answer. It is beyond answer. I wonder how anyone can live with themselves knowing they have done just that. How does one go home and explain to family members what they have done at work today, if not today, then when they go home on leave? More horrors await us as we are taken to see the gallows where twelve prisoners were hanged in the largest 'public' execution to take place in the camp. Finally we see a single gallows where the camp commandant Rudolph Hoss, not Hess, was hung for his war crimes on 16th April 1947.

Two hours have passed and we are taken on a free shuttle bus to Auschwitz II-Birkenhau. The mood is solemn. Not a word is spoken until the guide continues, once we have all made our way from the bus to this new site of horror.

'The Germans destroyed seven villages to build this death camp. Some of the wooden huts have been burnt down; the gas chambers have been partly destroyed but not completely destroyed. Come, let us continue.'

We walk down the infamous railway line and see one solitary cattle wagon.

'That has only been here a few years. An Australian businessman searched for one and found this one in another part of Europe. He paid for its restoration and the transportation to here. Why? It was because his father was a prisoner here. Who is he? He is the owner of a shopping mall. Did you know that Auschwitz was insured? Do you know which firm made the German uniforms?'

We are told the answers and both companies are still trading.

'Do you still want to deal with them?' we are asked. 'If they hadn't taken the contracts then someone else would. They were both small companies then.'

It is thought provoking stuff. We continue on, walking down the line to the end where there is a memorial to the dead. Either side of the line are two of the gas chambers that have been partly destroyed. They are cordoned off piles of rubble but still recognisable as to what they were as the Germans couldn't finish the job before departing. There are pools of water that are filled with human ashes, one of which is singled out to be representative. It has four memorial plaques with the same message. One in Polish, one in English, one in Hebrew and one in Yiddish.

We are taken into a wooden hut with communal toilets, which have a honeycomb of seats offering no privacy. There were some washbasins but they have been removed.

The dialogue continues. 'The prisoners were only allowed to use these facilities twice a day. Dysentery was rife and hygiene was a problem. One survivor who worked here told me that it saved her life as she could use the toilets when she needed to and also the washbasins, so basically shovelling shit saved her life.'

We move on to the barracks and, as in Auschwitz I, the bunk beds were three tiered.

'Which do you suppose was the best bunk to be in, top, middle or bottom?' we are asked.

Several answer and each position is favoured for different reasons; then comes the answer.

'So I am told, it was the top bunk,' says our guide. 'As I have already mentioned, the prisoners could only use the latrines twice a day; dysentery was rife and so quite literally they shit their pants. Now can you imagine being in the middle or bottom bunks and, well you can imagine can't you? Do you wonder why the facilities were so primitive? Remember this was a death camp, not a hotel. People did not survive too long here. Come back in winter when it is –25 °C and feel what it was like.'

We make our way back to the starting point of the visit of Auschwitz II still trying to take it all in. The site is so vast that one cannot see the extent of it all. Beyond the railway line and the gas chambers are some woods where there is another gas chamber that we don't get to see. The wood is silent. Everywhere is silent. There is no rustling of leaves, no snapping of twigs, nothing, not a sound. The silence is deafening.

As we prepare to leave our guide addresses us one last time. 'People ask me why I do this job and I tell them that it is personal. My great grandfather was one of the first Polish political prisoners in Auschwitz I, for seven months, until he was transferred elsewhere. He survived; if he hadn't then I wouldn't be here. My grandmother has been a guide for 38 years and I myself have been doing this for six years. Sometimes it gets emotional, especially when survivors return or when relatives of prisoners come here and tell me their stories. Every 14th June there is a man who visits. He is 93 years old now and the only living survivor of four men who acquired German uniforms, stole the camp commandant's car and drove out of Auschwitz I unchallenged. They were never caught. He is the only one still alive today. Of the other survivors who return, their numbers are getting less each year because of their age. One day there will be no one.

My colleague was taking some German-speaking visitors around and he pointed at a picture where the senior German officer, by a flick of the wrist determined the fate of the prisoner. One way meant death; the other way meant work. Next to that officer was another officer and standing a little apart was a third. One of the visitors looked at that third officer with horror. He had recognised his own father! He couldn't consult him on the matter as the father had died while he himself was quite young so he checked on his father's army record and found that he was the person in the picture. His mother and other close family members spoke very little on the matter. Did they know, I wonder? How did that man feel when he knew that it was his father?

I believe everybody in the world should come here to remind themselves of how cruel the human race can be. Look at the world today, it is happening again. Do we really want a repeat? Thank you for being here.'

It is hard to take it all in. We walk back to the bus stop. The drizzle has stopped but the whole scene is still without colour. Nobody speaks. There is a numbness that won't go away. It is meant to make an impression, and it does. Somehow four hours have passed while we were at the two sites yet time is an irrelevance while being here.

By mid afternoon we are back in Krakow. During the bus journey neither of us had spoken; we were still numb with the shock of what we had seen. We stop for a cappuccino and a slice of creamy, calorie-busting gateau and decide that we will explore the museum beneath Sukkennice (Cloth Hall), a massively impressive building taking up one side of Rynek Glowny, Europe's largest square. The museum tells the history of the city from the very early days through to the present day. There are plenty of touch screen displays giving information. There are plenty of models and in places perspex flooring which covers original walls of earlier buildings. There is so much to see and take in that several visits would be required to gain a complete understanding. It is a fabulous place to gather information for a school project. Two hours pass in the blink of an eye and the only reason we leave is because we have a dinner date with Lady F's 'man in Poland'.

After the total sadness of Auschwitz, a visit that I'm glad I've done, it is the perfect antidote to share a meal with them. This is their city so we suggest that they choose somewhere to eat. They recommend a Ukrainian restaurant, which doesn't look that good from the outside but inside is ideal. The menu is different from what we are used to yet with a little guidance we find that it is all rather good. We dine very well for very little money, about half what we'd spend at home, and naturally I have to try the Ukrainian vodka as well as two flavoured Polish vodkas.

Lady F and I still haven't done the family history chart; our minds haven't been on it, so that gives us a chance to meet up again. We arrange for a lunch date on the day of our departure. After a smashing evening we part company and Lady F and I head back to the apartment emotionally drained.

We are too slow getting up the stairs and the lights go out. We have failed to beat the timer and are plunged into darkness. While Lady F fumbles for the right key for the lock I grope around on the wall for the light switch, think I've found it and press it, only to find it is the doorbell to the adjoining apartment. After a bit more fumbling around by the light of a mobile phone (an after thought for a light source) we finally let ourselves in. It has been a long day!

Text to Junior: ***Visited Auschwitz. Mentally drained. Tried Ukrainian vodka.***

12-09-13

Yesterday was like no other that I have experienced and when I wake up I can still hear the chilling tales of Auschwitz. It has stopped raining though and Lady F is champing at the bit, ready to have another full day of site seeing. The destination today is Wieliczka and the salt mines. It is on the UNESCO World Heritage list so I am expecting great things. We catch an early bus, reach our destination and purchase our tickets. There are no stickers this time but we are still grouped together by language.

Our guide meets us and says, 'Good morning ladies and gentlemen. The mine has been worked here since the Middle Ages and only in recent times has production stopped. There are 400 miners still employed who maintain the tunnels. We are going to see just a fraction of the tunnels that stretch in total for 300 kilometres. The tunnels are on nine levels and we shall finish on the bottom layer, which is 327 metres below the surface, where you will find a café. You will be pleased to know that you do not have to climb up all the steps that we go down on the tour. There is a lift and you may use it when you wish after the tour has finished. Follow me please.'

Off we go into the underground world, leaving the warm air and sunshine behind. I lick my finger, rub it on a tunnel wall and taste the result. Unsurprisingly it is salty. I don't know why I should have expected anything different! The tunnels are larger than I thought they would be, almost as large as the tunnels on the London Underground network. We stop on three different levels and on each of these are statues carved out of salt that depict the way of life of the miners. The detail is astonishingly good. We are taken to a small lake, more pond size than lake and are told that it is saltier than the Dead Sea so that it wouldn't be possible to swim in it, not that I'd want to.

The highlight for me has to be the cathedral, a huge cavernous space that is adorned with salt chandeliers, statues and carvings. The two that catch my eye are a replica of 'The Last Supper' and also a scene of Joseph leading Mary with baby Jesus on the back of a donkey. Of all the statues, the most remarkable is a life-size carving of Pope John Paul II who, as Father Karol Wojtyla, lived in Krakow from 1951 until 1967. Weddings still take place in this cathedral and what a setting it must be for the occasion!

Moving on we see other notable figures from Poland's history and as we reach the café at the end of the tour an unbelievable three hours have passed. Even at this depth there is a souvenir shop that we have a cursory look at but purchase nothing. Lady F and I sit in the café and enjoy a cup of coffee, still marvelling at what we have seen. From here we make our way to the lift for the quick ascent to the surface and then catch the bus back to Krakow.

As the city is easily walkable we make our way to Wawel Castle on the other side of the city from the bus station. The castle is easy to find but looks like no castle that I have ever seen before. We pass through the gate and inside we see a cathedral, next to which is a castle but in truth looks more like a block of apartments in a quadrangle. In the grounds we find a model of the whole site and it confirms my suspicions that it looks like a walled fortification for a very select group of people in days gone by.

We look inside the cathedral and I find the statues and décor just too much. It is almost like it has been over done to impress. I learn later that this is the place where the kings of Poland were crowned so I suppose that it is the Polish equivalent of Westminster Abbey.

I find a tower to climb and it is well worth it for the views over the River Vistula that flows through the city on its way to a delta estuary before entering the Baltic Sea near Gdansk. Away from the river there are splendid views over the city. While I am up here on my lofty perch I overhear two ladies with Scottish accents discussing their trip so far. It sounds similar to the one I am doing with Lady F, the only difference being that we are visiting the same landmarks as they are but in a different order. My eavesdropping has given me another piece of information and that is where the Jewish quarter is. Despite the horrors of the past, that were graphically illustrated yesterday, the Jewish community is beginning to blossom again. Somewhere in the direction that they are pointing is the Oskar Schindler factory that has now been turned into a museum and is another place that I'd like to visit, but sadly it will have to wait for another time. Already I have fallen into my old habit of finding more things to do than I have time to do them in. Lady F agrees with me.

As we make our way down the tower and out of the castle grounds, we see a man in national costume pedalling his bicycle with a bag of shopping on the handlebars. He is certainly a colourful character but where he has come from or where he is going to I have no idea.

Lady F decides that we must go to a restaurant called Chlopski Jadto for our evening meal. The place comes highly recommended but we have difficulty finding it. After much footslogging and a bit of prompting from the locals we eventually get there. The name translates as Farmers Food although Lady F remembers the name as Chopsticks because it's easier to say. Inside it has a rustic look to it. The tables and chairs are made of solid wood that have been worn shiny in places so must be old. I wonder what stories they could tell! We share a huge platter of meat and assorted vegetables, which I wash down with a Polish lager and a couple of vodkas, while Lady F settles for water. I am getting a liking for the local vodka. Memo to self: 'be careful, it is strong stuff'. We spend a couple of very pleasant hours going over the day and generally talking about how much we have packed into a short time.

'I'll tell you something Lady F, if ever I come back to Krakow, and I do hope I will, I would like to come here again for another meal. The food has been excellent wherever we've been but I think this is the best yet.'

'I'll go along with that,' she replies.

We pay the bill and walk back to the apartment. It has been another full day. We climb the stairs quicker now to beat the time switch, although we press the light switch on each floor to give us more time. It is strange how one gets the hang of things just when it is time to leave.

Text to Junior: *Went to salt mines and Wawel castle. All is well. Haven't got lost ... yet!*

13-09-13

It is a strange start to the day. Every time I look out of the window the weather seems to change. One minute it is bright and sunny, the next there are dark clouds and drizzle. We pack our bags, do a sweep of the apartment then walk to the agency and hand the keys in.

The next thing we do is to go shopping and get a present for Nettie, my dear wife who declined this trip. I hate shopping. Lady F is indifferent about it but decides that she really ought to purchase a souvenir or two. We make our way to the shopping mall and I start to look. There is so much to choose from that in the end I find there is too much and I get confused. Lady F takes a more measured approach and eventually buys something. I ask her advice and her opinions narrow the choices for me. I'm getting irritable now so in a rash moment I make my choice, buy it and decide that it is 'job done'. Lady F is still browsing! What is it that women find so fascinating about shopping? I'm certain that the shopkeepers don't know either but they do encourage it by providing bench seats in between the rows of shops for the brow-beaten, disillusioned men folk to sit upon, to save them trudging round from store to store. That leaves the women free to browse unhindered. They know where their men are should they need an opinion, but more likely some more money!

I actually see one man sitting on a bench looking downhearted, round-shouldered and forlorn. He looks ready to end it all as his wife and daughters make regular trips with bags of shopping and use him as a dumping ground, then go back to shop for more. I feel sorry for him. I want to yell at the women and ask them how they are going to carry all the bags to the car. I'm working up a mental frenzy when Lady F startles me.

'Fancy a coffee?'

'What?' I say as I'm fast-tracked back to reality.

'Coffee? You're miles away. Where have you been?'

'It's best that you don't know,' I reply as I hastily make my way out of the shopping mall, then breathe a sigh of relief as we head across the square and pick an outside seat at a fashionable restaurant. We just have time to drink our coffees when Lady F points to a figure striding across the square towards us.

'What is his name?' I ask Lady F.

'Who?'

'Him, your man in Poland, I can't remember what he said,' I say as I discreetly as I can while pointing to the figure approaching us.

'Cooper, I think; it's something like that.'

'Don't you know?'

'I'm sure it is.'

'Good day Cooper,' I say. 'How are you?'

'Very well, thank you. Did you enjoy the shopping?

'Don't ask!'

'I understand, I have the same problem. Now where shall we go for lunch?'

'You know the city better than we do so we'll leave it to you,' says Lady F.

We are taken to a restaurant that excels in local cuisine just off the main square. The food is simple fare but good quality and filling. As this is lunch I decline a vodka, even though it is our last day here and settle for a beer instead.

'Cooper, here is the chart that we promised you. I have filled in some names from Lady F's family tree so with what you know of your family tree and the papers that Lady F has given you, you can see where, if at all, your families link up. To help you further these are first cousins, these are second cousins, third cousins etc. These are first cousins once removed, twice removed, second cousins once removed, twice removed etc. The removed bit is just a generation thing,' I say as I point out on the chart the descriptions

I give him. Once you have put in all your names then you can see how you link up with Lady F, if indeed you do.'

Cooper is silent for a moment then says to me, 'You know Jay; that makes a lot of sense. You've explained it very well.'

'Excellent. You can keep the chart if you wish.'

'Thank you; now as we have a bit of time we can either visit the Schindler museum but we won't have time to see it all, or we can walk to the river, whatever you like.'

We choose to walk to the river because the one thing we don't want to do is to have one eye on the clock if we are going to the Schindler museum. Cooper then becomes our tour guide as we walk to the Jewish Quarter.

'This road that we are now walking on is the boundary between the Jewish community and the Christian community. It's not really a demarcation zone, it's just that Jews live on one side and Christians on the other.'

We enter the Jewish area.

'This area is really starting to smarten itself up after years of neglect. Even as recently as five years ago you really wouldn't want to be walking around here after dark. It wasn't a very nice place. It is alright now though.'

We can see what he means. There is a definite sign of buildings being smartened up. There is a way to go yet but it looks to be progressing.

Soon we are at the river and there is a twin crossing. There is one bridge for pedestrians, one for bicycles and nothing for cars. My eye is drawn to the wire mesh attached to the lower level of railings on both crossings as they are covered in padlocks. There are plenty of them and the difference between these and others that I have seen in other cities in other countries is that these have the names of the people written on them and are dated; others have been engraved. Someone has even attached a bicycle lock!

A paddle steamer passes underneath the bridge on a pleasure cruise. Cooper laughs.

'What's so funny about a paddle steamer?' I ask him.

'Not that; this,' he says pointing to a padlock. 'It is two female names and this one is two boys names and who would be in love with a bicycle? It takes all sorts I suppose.'

'It's a great idea. It's a harmless bit of fun and it adds a bit of character to the place. I don't suppose the authorities are too concerned because some of these locks are quite rusty. I agree with you on one thing though.'

'What's that?'

'Who loves a bicycle more than a woman or a man, depending who put it there?'

'Come on, it's time to go to the airport. The traffic is building up and there are roadworks along the way.'

We climb in the car and Cooper gets us to the airport in good time. He is quite right about the roadworks and has allowed himself enough time to deal with it. I'm sorry to be leaving. It has been a wonderful few days and there is still more to do.

'I wouldn't mind coming back here again, sooner rather than later,' I say to Lady F.

'Like wise.'

We make our way through formalities to wait for our flight.

'Do you know something? For once I wouldn't have minded being frisked at the security check. You know my luck, I nearly always get singled out as the random choice and yet when there is a good looking young lady I miss out!'

'You're getting worse you are!'

'Yep!'

'What would your wife say?'

'Nettie?'

'Who else?'

'I've got a problem with her. You remember how Cooper said that I was good at explaining myself, well I can't actually remember telling her how long I'd be away for.'

'What!'

'I'll phone her when we get to Stansted and we'll find out. It'll either be a lift home or a long walk.'

'If she isn't there then you *will* have some explaining to do.'

'I know.'

The flight is another 'on time flight' and we pass through passport control fairly quickly. I phone my good lady and as luck would have it she is waiting for us at the airport.

'We've got a lift home. Nettie is waiting for us,' I say, mightily relieved.

'What was your problem?' asks Lady F.

'I must have had a senior moment because apparently I had left all the flight details with her and for the life of me couldn't remember doing so. I need a holiday!'

Text to Junior: ***Still alive. Didn't get lost. Had a great time. Back in England.***

Christmas Markets in Northern Italy

As luck would have it Nettie has the same thoughts. She also feels the need to get away before Christmas and she booked this trip up before telling me. Fed up with trying to get me motivated into the Christmas spirit she has an inspired idea.

'We are going to Italy for a few days. We will be staying in Arco, northern Italy and visiting the Christmas markets in Verona, Merano and Bolzano as well as the one in Arco,' she announces.

Now I know why she didn't tell me before hand. Too many hours at work were taking their toll on her and she didn't fancy the idea of me arguing. As if.......!

'You do know how cold it's going to be don't you?' I say.

'Of course.'

'I didn't think you liked the cold.'

'I don't.'

'So why choose somewhere cold when you don't like the cold?'

'Because it's Christmas.'

'It's November!'

'It'll be December when we're there and that's Christmas month. And we're doing lots of shopping in the Christmas markets so cold doesn't come into it.'

'Are you taking a suitcase or just hand luggage?' I ask, having already decided that the good lady loves the thought of five days of shopping.

'A suitcase of course, the package allows us one case each.'

'What is the weight limit?' I ask, wondering just how much this pack mule will have to carry.

'Twenty-three kilograms.'

'Each?'

'Yes'

'That's nearly half a hundredweight each! How am I supposed to carry all that?'

'You're not. We'll take one suitcase between the two of us, and one piece of hand luggage each. Happy?'

'Delirious,' I say flatly.

'You worry too much. We can always get another suitcase out there if we need to.' Nettie assures me.

'Twenty-three kilos is a limit not a target my dear.'

'If you say so,' she replies, smiling that smile which says she is taking no notice of me. 'Look excited then,'

'I am excited but my face hasn't got the message yet.'

30-11-13

The day arrives and as we have an afternoon flight from Gatwick we don't have to make an early start from home. We enjoy a leisurely drive to the North Terminal car park, find plenty of space to park in and then catch the shuttle bus. There are no crowds to worry about as we check-in, wait to board the plane, and then enjoy a smooth flight to Verona Airport.

From there we board a coach and enjoy the one-hour drive to the hotel in Arco. Our tour guide, a middle-aged lady with tied back blonde hair and a large, thick black overcoat is giving us a talk about where we are going and what we will see during our stay but the beautiful scenery and the grapevines in the valley distract me. I hope Nettie is paying attention to the talk because if it comes to 'question time', I will be found wanting.

A constant source of fascination for me is the different methods of training the vines. Some have been tied up in a linear method, which is quite common in wine growing regions but some here have been trained on 'Y' shaped frames. Harvesting them has to be done by hand as the pickers walk underneath the wires and snip the hanging bunches of grapes. I can't see how mechanical harvesting would be possible.

Darkness descends, blocking out the vines as we approach the town of Arco. The next thing we know is that we have arrived at our hotel. The temperature has dropped close to zero. We check into our room and stay put for the evening.

01-12-13

After a comfortable night sleep and a continental breakfast we make our way out of the hotel for the coach trip to Verona where we will wander around the Christmas Market and also some historical sites, if I can prise the good lady away from the market! As we step out of the hotel the scene is one of postcards and travel brochures. There is a bright blue sky and mountains that look like icing sugar has been sprinkled on them. The sun is warm on the face, it brightens the day and it all bodes well for what lays ahead.

As the coach speeds us along the motorway, I am still drawn to the endless acres of vines. I watch as men, in several layers of clothing, are going about the thankless task of pruning, ready for next year's growth. It all seems a far cry from the heat of summer, the swelling of the grapes and the frenetic activity at harvest time. I am poked in the ribs by Nettie and take it as a sign to listen as the guide tells us a little bit about Verona and the immediate area.

'The city straddles the Adage River and the architecture has gained it UNESCO World Heritage status. There is a Roman amphitheatre built around 30 AD, which is the third largest in Italy, and we will walk past it as I take you into the market stall area. The city is also the setting for three of William Shakespeare's plays, "Romeo and Juliet", "Two Gentlemen of Verona" and "The Taming of the Shrew". You have maps that I have given you and all the landmarks are marked on them. There are many more that I haven't mentioned but it is the market that you have come to see today. Maybe you will come back and see some of the other places on another holiday.

The balcony that Juliet is supposed to have stood on is a popular site so allow yourselves plenty of time to see it, if that is what you wish to do as well as the market. We will get off the coach here, by the old city wall, so if you get lost just head for this wall and follow it back to here.'

We are led to the market stall area and start to explore. The wooden huts display an impressive array of Christmas bits and pieces for the tree and around the house. There are a number of nativity scenes, each one more impressive than the last. It is a conundrum as to know where to start. Just as I am flagging on the shopping front I am taken by surprise when Nettie puts a suggestion to me that doesn't involve shopping.

'Let's go up the Torre dei Lamberti (Lamberti Tower),' she says.

I readily agree as the good lady knows that I love climbing towers or going into tunnels. I'm just surprised that she has torn herself away from shopping but I'm not going to question it!

We pay our money to enter the medieval tower, which at eighty-four metres tall is the largest in Verona, and while Nettie takes the lift, I climb the 243 steps to where the lift stops. I meet her there and together we climb forty-six more steps to another platform where hangs a large bell. From there it is another seventy-nine steps to the highest point that we can go. The views are magnificent, the houses are packed close together but the distinctive feature is the turrets that are on top of some walls and towers. While the sides are straight, the middle is shaped like a fish tail, a sort of curved 'V' and that is indicative of the influence of the House of La Scala, so we find out later. Looking down to the piazza, it is noticeable that it is becoming ever more crowded, as do the adjoining streets, so we decide to descend the steps and go in search of Juliet's house that is nearby.

It is easy enough to find but I am shocked to see just how much graffiti is on the short tunnel walls that lead into the courtyard. There is so much of it that it can be argued that it is an art form in it's own right. The courtyard is crowded but I do manage to see on the wall opposite the entrance an area devoted to lover's padlocks, a feature that seems to be springing up in cities all over the place. It is something that I am rather fond of but next to it is something that I hope never catches on. It is a wall of chewing gum. After chewing the gum it is then stuck to a wall and initials carved into the gooey mess. I just find it disgusting.

I fear that I may have been lost in the moment for too long because when I turn to speak to Nettie, she isn't there. I look this way and that without success, then I hear her distinctive voice calling, 'Romeo, Romeo, wherefore art though Romeo?'

The screech at the end of the last 'Romeo' has me wincing. The crowd look up at the balcony and then, it seems everyone is looking at me. Why me I wonder? And then I look nervously up at the balcony. There before my eyes is my beloved wife, dressed in a red flowerpot hat and tweed jacket, with her arms held out in a ten-to-two position leaning slightly over the balcony. Our eyes meet and she just grins at me. I look away and wonder if this is exactly what Shakespeare had in mind when he penned those immortal words. I look up again and she has gone. The next thing I am aware of is Nettie having crept up on me, grabbing me by the arm and whispering softly in my ear, 'How was that for you darling?' and plants a kiss on my cheek.

'Unforgettable, my dear, truly unforgettable,' I reply.

The crowd is increasing as we fight our way out of the courtyard and find that it is no better outside on the street. It seems that the world and his wife have descended on Verona. I am getting close to pavement rage as people constantly stop in front of me or else bump into me because they are walking in one direction while looking in another. We agree to find a seat at an outside table at one of the many restaurants and cafes around the piazza, have a coffee and watch the madness of the human race. I am surprised at how little, if any, actual shopping has been done, unless of course it is like training for a marathon, and pacing oneself is the key.

We take a slow walk back to the coach and it feels like everyone else is going in the opposite direction. Quite how crowded the centre of Verona will be in a couple of hours doesn't bear thinking about.

The drive back to Arco is even better than the morning drive as we leave the motorway early and take the scenic route alongside Lake Garda. It takes us along a stretch of road that was used in one of the James

Bond films. We are told how many cars were written off and how the finished scene appeared in the film. While that may be of interest to some, I prefer not to know. I just want to enjoy the finished article in the same way that I do not wish to know how a magician does his tricks.

Back in Arco and mindful that I have been told that no purchases have been made I am led to the Christmas Market just a couple of minutes from the hotel. There is a laser advent calendar being projected onto the walls of the surrounding buildings. Stallholders are cheerful and there is a very seasonal atmosphere. By now it is dark, the temperature has dropped noticeably and so I feel it is incumbent upon me to sample some of the local gluhwein. It has a rounded fruity flavour to it. It is warming parts of me that have started to freeze and so I feel the sensible thing to do is have another glass to build up my resistance to the cold night air.

As I am enjoying the second glassful, Nettie announces that she has made a purchase and would like to celebrate the occasion with a cup of tea at the hotel, thereby denying me a third glass. She is also feeling the cold. It is a sensible move on two counts, one is that shopping has been halted for the day and the other is that we will both stay warm in the hotel. On the short walk back I am thinking that we have spent all day at two markets and only one purchase has been made. At this rate the twenty-three kilogram limit is safe. I keep those thoughts to myself and smile.

'What are you smiling about?' asks Nettie.

'Just thinking about you on the balcony in Verona

my dear. It was one of those moments that will stay with me forever.'

'That's nice,' she whispers.

So was the gluhwein, but say nothing.

02-12-13

Another glorious day of blue skies and sunshine greet us as we step outside for the first time today. The snow on the mountaintops has receded just a little but the scene is still beautiful enough to put a smile on our faces. Our plan for today is to climb the hill behind the hotel and visit the medieval castle perched on top of the limestone cliff. A charming New Zealand lady who cannot persuade her husband to walk up the hill and who doesn't wish to go alone accompanies us. When we meet her in the foyer she is wearing an identical tweed jacket to Nettie. I fear there will be friction but it is an ill-founded fear, as both ladies start chattering away like long lost friends. Walking behind them causes me a few anxious moments as, occasionally; I think that I may be suffering from double vision!

The pathway is steep in places and with the early morning dew still clinging to the stones, a little slippery. At each and every opportunity, where there is a clear view of the Sarca Valley, we stop and take some pictures. The air is crisp and clear but as the morning wears on and the heat rises, so does the mist, which hangs in the valley and spoils a good picture.

Eventually we reach a hut and hire an audio set that explains the different points when we reach them. It is both fascinating and informative in equal measure as we move from one point to the next. Restoration is still going on which means that some areas are temporarily out of bounds. Frescos, hundreds of years old are still visible on the interior walls, each telling a story.

Until now the only other human contact we have had is with one man attending to some nets under the olive trees and the castle staff. There are no other visitors. It is a refreshing and pleasant change from the scrum in Verona.

When we get as close to the top as it's possible to get I look around a rock and downwards to see the valley disappear into the distance. A river runs to one side of it and there are grapevines for as far as the eye can see. All the houses, of which there are only a few, have worked the land adjoining them. No piece of land is wasted. It is yet another scene of breathtaking beauty.

We take more pictures and then start on the descent. It is harder than the climb because of the angle of the slope. It causes the calf muscles to shorten and cramp. The knee joints take a bit of jarring as we are constantly checking ourselves against the gathering momentum, which would have us running down the slope out of control. It is only when we are halfway down do we see the first sign of anyone going where we have just been. The numbers increase as we near the town and we conclude that we chose the best time of day to visit the castle.

The New Zealand lady thanks us for our company and we go our separate ways. She has been a delight to be with.

'Let's walk along the riverside to Riva after lunch,' says Nettie, who is constantly surprising me.

'Are you sure about this,' I ask nervously.

'Of course, I like walking at a leisurely pace.'

'Then why don't you do some more walking at home?'

'Because it's always to the same places near home and I get bored. Here I'm on holiday, it's different and there are no distractions.'

While Nettie is in the mood we find the footpath, which doubles as a cycle lane and is marked red, and we follow it to the river. The green sign outside the pharmacy is showing 13 °C, which is well above what is normally expected at this time of year. It is our good fortune. The sun makes our faces glow and soon we are warm enough to unbutton our coats. As with our walk to the castle, this morning, there are not too many people about.

Gardens are full of leafless trees and barren earth where crops have been harvested and the soil is resting before being made ready for the new season. Nowhere do we see neglected gardens. The river rushes over small rocks on its urgent journey to spill into Lake Garda. We catch our first glimpse of the lake and then find a café suitably placed at the end of the footpath. We sit at an outside table and rest our weary legs while slowly drinking our cappuccinos. I then watch with some incredulity as a woman at a nearby table gets up, takes her cigarettes with her as she enters the café and leaves a camera, unguarded on the table.

Suitably refreshed, we pay the bill and walk the short distance to the lake. We are just in time to see the sun setting behind the mountain and casting a shadow over the golden leaves of the lakeside trees. We continue to watch as the shadow progresses remorselessly on, devouring anything and everything in its way, as it slowly advances up the mountainside on the other side of the lake. The temperature drops by 5°C in as many minutes. Coats are buttoned up and our walking speeds up as we head off into town to see what it has to offer. Most of the town of Riva is pedestrianised which is a delight for us as we can wander freely from one side of the street to the other without fear of traffic. The street decorations are every bit as good as we have seen elsewhere and all the shops have made an effort. It creates a very good seasonal atmosphere. I buy four postcards and stamps ready to send them to friends at home who keep track of my wanderings.

Ever mindful of the time we catch one of the last buses of the day back to Arco. It has been a very rewarding day as we have gone at our own pace and done everything we set out to do. Before dinner we try some of the hotels' own wine and then after dinner I have a grappa with my cappuccino. Nettie is engaged in conversation with the New Zealand lady. There is a lot of laughing going on between themselves and other women in the group. I'm on my guard, as are their husbands, with the prospect of another two markets to visit tomorrow.

03-12-13

At 03-00 I am woken up by the sound of the television broadcasting the world news. Nettie cannot sleep. Too much walking, as well as the prospect of more shopping has got her twitchy. When she can't sleep, she turns the television on with the volume up too loud and that wakes me. Unbelievably, I then receive a text message. I know it isn't from Junior because he knows better than to text me in the middle of the night. Come to think of it he never sends me a text when I'm out of England because he thinks alien forces are at work and they will trace the message to his fortress and abduct him. I look at the number but I don't recognise it. I send a message back only to find that the sender has a wrong number.

After a few more hours of fitful sleep I wake up properly, enjoy a hearty continental breakfast and board the coach for the trip to Merano and Bolzano for two more Christmas Markets. I can hardly wait! On the way we are given a briefing by our guide. 'In the north of Italy, where we are going today, German is widely spoken and there are some residents who resent the Italian language being spoken. The road signs are in both languages and in some small villages three languages are used. The third language is Ladin, which is an offshoot of Latin. The story is that a legion of Roman soldiers was abandoned in the mountains, settled down and a community was formed. Their language was Ladin and it was passed down through the generations. It is still spoken in some parts today. It has now been officially recognised and is taught in schools in the Trentino and South Tyrol regions.'

I turn to Nettie and say, 'She's a mine of information and I'm enjoying the history lessons as much as anything else.'

'You would do, anything to take your mind off of shopping. Have you got my present yet?'

'No, I'm still looking,' I reply, as if I'd tell her! I remember one year when I did admit to having bought her present well before the big day, ten days before actually, it was pandemonium. She behaved like a six year old, turning the house upside down looking for it. So now I say nothing at all even if it means being economical with the truth!

We are on another drive through spectacular scenery as we head towards Merano, which is famous for its spas, not that we are likely to have time to visit any when there are rows of festive wooden huts to browse. The air is so still that white smoke from the chimney of a nearby building leaves the stack and ascends vertically without deviation.

'Look at that,' says Nettie pointing to the smoke. 'What do you suppose that building is?'

'Somewhere where they chose a new pope? Because it is the only building with white smoke coming out of it,' I reply flippantly. 'Don't know,' would have been a better answer judging by the frosty look I am now getting.

Once again the stalls are packed with tree decorations and tasty morsels to eat but at a price. To decorate a five-foot tree from scratch one could easily spend €200 and still have plenty of room left to fill. A better option would be to start with a small tree, build the collection of ornaments over the years and buy bigger trees each Christmas. For me the great delight is to see that the Nativity scene is promoted as the main event, which is after all, why we celebrate Christmas.

This is the third market that we have visited and so far my patience has held firm. I see a stall selling snacks so I try out my rusty German, ever mindful of what our guide has told us.

'Eine bratwurst bitte.'

'Are you English mate?'

'Yes.'

'Here you go. Enjoy.'

'Danke.'

'Have a nice day,' he cheerily replies, as I go on my way.

So much for speaking German I thought. I wonder if he would have been so accommodating had I spoken in Italian?

Our time here passes in a flash. There is so much more to see and do but shopping is the theme of the day and another market awaits us in Bolzano. We board the coach once more and head the short distance to Bolzano, which is only nineteen miles inside the Italian border.

Our guide continues the history lesson, 'Before World War One Bolzano was part of Austria but after the war it was annexed by Italy. On 1st January 1927 it became a provincial capital. Mussolini set about changing the area from a German speaking one to an Italian speaking one by allowing German speakers who didn't wish to become Italian to relocate and encouraged Italian citizens to move north. The German speakers that stayed were forced to learn Italian as all signs and notices were changed to Italian. Nowadays both languages are used but there are those descendents of the original inhabitants who still hate the Italian language, as they don't see it as their mother tongue. Don't be surprised if you get a cool reception if you try and speak Italian.

During World War Two Bolzano was the site of a transit camp for Jews and political prisoners. It is also the town where Otzi is housed in a museum. He was the iceman who was found in the mountains in the 1990's, I forget the exact year, but the museum is a few minutes walk from the market should you wish to visit it.'

My ears prick up at that piece of information and as the coach pulls into the parking bay, the shopaholics make a hasty exit and head to the market. We are two of the last to leave the coach and follow on. The stalls are every bit as good as what we have already seen but there is nothing new so I turn to Nettie and say, 'Shall we go to the museum and visit Otzi?'

'No,' she replies. 'I want to look at the stalls and the shops. You go by yourself.'

So I do. It is a relief to get away from shopping but part of me worries that the piece of plastic that is her 'flexible friend' may have to become a contortionist.

Also I fear that the twenty-three kilogram flight allowance maybe under threat. I decide to live dangerously and let her loose.

The museum is easy to find and surprisingly it is devoted entirely to Otzi. The man himself can be seen through the small window of his sealed climate controlled cell. His skin is shiny, like the glaze on some fruit tarts. All of his features are visible and it is astonishing to think that he has been dated to about 6,000 years old. He was found by chance in 1991 as melting snow receded to uncover his body. The find quickly caught the imagination of the world but being so close to the border both Austria and Italy claimed him as theirs. In the mountain areas the borders are a little bit fluid as nobody ventures too far off the beaten track but this find changed all that. The border had to be redrawn with a sharper pencil and it was found that Otzi was ninety-four metres inside the Italian border.

Further searches in the immediate area by archaeologists revealed his weapons and clothing. Otzi continues to fascinate scientists the world over. Examination of the body shows that he died from blood loss caused by an arrow shot into a blood vessel in his shoulder. It is thought that he did not die immediately as there are other wounds on his body so maybe it was a slow and painful death. Speculation continues as to whether he was part of a group or a loner. No one knows for sure.

Several student groups are being escorted around the museum having the story explained to them. If asked to write an essay on how Otzi came to be where he was and speculate about whether he was a loner or not then the students could let their imaginations flow freely. Any well written logical argument should gain high marks because there is no definitive correct answer, only speculation and probabilities. How many will rise to the challenge I wonder?

I look at the clothes, arrows and other artefacts that have been unearthed and I am astonished at how good the condition is considering the age of them. Two Dutchmen have produced a computer-generated image of how Otzi might have looked and spookily, his face looks like someone I know. I just can't put a name to him yet!

I am totally absorbed with all the details when I hear a whining sound. My ears prick up. I know that sound; it's Nettie's 'flexible friend' being asked to bend just a little bit further. He needs rescuing. I look at my watch and realise that I'm over the time that I said I'd be. I'm late for my rendez-vous with the good lady. She is bound to be worried, at least I like to think that she will be worried, but I expect the truth is that she is as lost in her world of shopping as I am in Otzi's.

I leave the museum and start making my way to our agreed meeting place, when a shop that seems to specialise in selling Nativity scenes distracts me. From the smallest to the largest they are all well made with plenty of fine detail but there is one that disturbs me. It seems to be a collision between the Nativity scene as described in the Bible and Noah's Ark. There are just too many different animals, even though the whole scene does look good.

I find Nettie laden with gifts looking pleased with herself. Before I have a chance to speak she says, 'I've found a drink that you really ought to try. You will like it, I do.'

'What is it?'

'White gluhwein.'

'Never heard of it,' I say. 'I thought gluhwein was only made with red wine.'

'Neither had I but it's very drinkable.'

So I try a mug of the seasonal beverage and the good lady is right. Why do I ever doubt her? It is so good and warming that I'm compelled to have another. I am almost halfway through the second mug when I realise, too late of course, that this is a softening up process before she tells me just how successful her shopping has been without me! Her beaming face is such a joy to behold that I haven't got the heart to mention the twenty-three kilogram limit. Then comes a bombshell.

'I should have brought Princess with me instead of you; she would have loved it here with all the shopping. Think of all the fun we could have.'

I'm thinking and I can hear a whimper from her 'flexible friend' begging me not to allow it!

We take a last look at the stalls before boarding the coach for the drive back to Arco. It is dark now and I doze on and off, reflecting on how I have survived four Christmas Markets in four days and not become irritable.

Back at the hotel after dinner I am content to sit and chat with the other male survivors of the shopping experience when Nettie tells me that she has discovered a Nativity trail around the houses and wants to explore. The New Zealand lady wants to go with her but they don't want to go alone down dark narrow side streets so I am pressed into service as a chaperone. The other husband doesn't even get asked. Oh lucky me! Each house along the route has a scene of some sort displayed outside; some are very good, while others are rubbish. Nettie and her tweed-coated twin, a few glasses of wine the worse for wear try and photograph every single one of them. I am getting cold watching this pointless activity. We are going round in circles and just as I think about grumbling we come back to the hotel from a different direction.

Another grappa, another cappuccino and I thaw out. It has been a memorable day for one reason or another but I dread to think what the women will think of the pictures they took in the sober light of tomorrow morning.

04-12-13

Unbelievably we wake up to yet another glorious day of blue skies and sunshine. Nettie is in whimsical mood as she says to me over breakfast, 'I think we ought to look around the market here again, don't you?'

'Why?' I ask.

'Because I haven't seen it in daylight.'

'What difference does that make?'

'I might have missed something,' she tells me.

'Unlikely,' I reply. 'There's not much gets past you.'

'You don't understand do you?'

'No sweetheart I don't,' I say.

No man understands women in shopping mode and I'm no different but as there is a cut off point, because it's departure day, I take the initiative, 'We'd better get going,' I say and that throws Nettie completely off guard.

She soon recovers, realises that I'm not joking and is soon away from the breakfast table and setting the pace down the road to the market. We dawdle through the stalls in the sunshine and hurry through those in the shade. At the end of the first circuit I make the mistake of thinking that the shopping trip has ended, but it hasn't. We start on a second circuit and Nettie makes some purchases. When we reach the end of the lap I resign myself to the fact that there will be a third, but no; the good lady makes a comment that is music to my ears, music to any man's ears in similar circumstances.

'I've finished shopping,' she declares with a huge smile and waves her latest purchase at me.

I daren't ask what it is in case it encourages another lap of the stalls. If I declare too much interest then maybe Nettie will think that I have missed something so I keep my acknowledgement simple and to the point. 'Lovely,' I say. 'Well done.'

We make our way back to the hotel and the suitcase gets repacked. Everything is squeezed in and then comes the weigh-in. The scales are hooked on, a button pressed and the case lifted up. Beyond my wildest dreams I read the digital read out and it is 22.3 kilograms; that is 0.7 kilos inside the limit. I read it again and the figure is the same, 700 grams inside the limit. I daren't ask about the hand luggage, I'm just happy that the suitcase is packed and legal.

To celebrate this momentous occasion we take one last walk by the river. I still cannot take in just how beautiful it is here. The sports stadium with its football pitch surrounded by a running track set in a valley covered with grapevines and overlooked by a medieval castle is breathtaking. Just to be involved with a club based here would be enough for me. Nettie sees the glazed look in my eyes and gently nudges me back to reality.

'Lunch,' she whispers and guides me back to the town.

We find exactly the cosy, intimate place we are looking for and enter. We are the first diners to be admitted for lunch and while we peruse the menu, several more follow us in. During our three-course meal we chat about many things and decide that this will be our main meal of the day. The idea of saving room for a chicken wrap on the plane doesn't warrant a second thought.

The time passes too quickly, when we would have preferred to linger, but we have to go back to the hotel. One last sweep of the room and we close the door for the last time. It is a pity. There is more to see and do here but for that I think a visit earlier in the year would be better. This is after all a Christmas Market holiday.

Our flight back arrives early, the case is on the carousel waiting for us as we pass through passport control and we are on the shuttle bus to the car park within twenty minutes of landing. The car journey is equally smooth and as I back the car onto the driveway Nettie turns to me and says, 'Do you know what? Princess would have loved this short break; maybe we should bring her next time.'

I say nothing. I treat it as a rhetorical question. It is the 'we' that disturbs me. Am I expected to spend five days shopping with TWO women!

Christmas

Total immersion in the Christmas markets has a lasting affect on me. I manage to get all my shopping done, cards written and posted, parcels wrapped and I still have a day to spare. It is almost unprecedented. I am ready for Christmas.

25-12-13

My phone bleeps, indicating a text message has arrived. It is from Junior.

'Call me. It is urgent.'

I know it isn't urgent because if it were, he'd have phoned me. He uses 'urgent' when he means 'important' but 'important' has too many letters, so he uses 'urgent' instead. I call Junior and he answers on the second ring.

'What's up?' I ask in my cheery manner.

'I need to talk to you. It's important,' he says in a whispered voice.

'Talk to me now, I'm listening.'

'I can't, it's too important. Can you call round please?'

'Okay, I'm on my way,' I say wearily. I've no idea what is troubling his over-active brain but he does have these moments from time to time.

I drive to his fortified mansion and find the tradesman's entrance, my usual way in, is undergoing extensive refurbishment so I have to use the main driveway. I wait at the impressive, almost intimidating wrought iron gates and have to go through exhaustive security checks before the gates finally swing open and I'm allowed to proceed. I drive up the gravel driveway at a sedate pace so as not to disturb the gravel too much, Junior hates wheel spins that disturb the order of stones, and I arrive at the front door. There are a few more security questions to answer before I'm allowed in. He has CCTV installed but he doesn't trust the images. At last we are face to face.

'Thanks for coming over so quickly,' he says breathlessly.

'My pleasure Junior, now what's the problem? What has got you worked up into such a state?'

'It's a song I've heard. It's called "Change at Thorpe-le-Soken for Walton-on-the-Naze". While I was listening to it I thought of you and how you left us all at Nice airport, caught a shuttle bus to the other terminal, changed buses and met us at the other end.'

'I know the song but what on earth has my taking the cheaper option of travel got to do with it?' I ask, curiosity now getting the better of me.

'Don't you see? People actually get off one train and on to another; you changed buses. I thought that was almost unheard of. I mean, if I don't drive to a place, I get a bus or take a train that does go there. Changing part of the way is something that has never occurred to me. Listening to the song changed all that.'

'You've brought me all this way to tell me that you've been to Liverpool Street station, caught a train and changed at Thorpe-le-Soken for Walton-on-the-Naze.'

'Good Lord no: I'm not that brave. What I did was to drive to Thorpe-le-Soken and caught the train directly to Walton-on-the-Naze just to see what was there.'

'And what was there?' I ask.

'I'm not really sure. I was going to explore but I was worried about getting lost and becoming stranded so I didn't get far. The station is at one of the highest points and it is possible to see all over the town from there. I could see two towers and when I came back home I researched them.'

'Why exactly have you called me over here?'

'I would like to do the train journey with you and then walk to the tower which looks like it's on the far side of town.'

'When?'

'Now, if that's alright with you. I need to get things straight in my head about navigating. Listening to the song about getting lost on the underground and wanting to get back to Liverpool Street; I've done that;

I've been lost on the underground and I've no idea how I got out of there and back home. It has unnerved me.'

Junior's voice is cracking as the memories make him emotional. Still I listen to him as he continues.

'The thing is, if you come with me, you can help me beat the demons in my head.'

'You're being a bit dramatic about this aren't you?'

'Please!' he begged, as he grabbed my arm.

'Okay, but how many times have you had a go at me about my navigating?'

'I know, I know, you do make a fist of it and take a while to do the simplest of things. You take wrong turnings and generally pick every wrong way before you get the right way but here's the thing; you do get there in the end. Anyone who can navigate out of Paris by the sun and a compass must be doing something right. You must have some sense of where you are and you aren't afraid of getting it wrong or getting lost. So, will you come with me by train from Thorpe-le-Soken to Walton-on-the-Naze, walk to the tower on the far side of town and back again explaining, along the way, how you navigate?'

'Is that some sort of back-handed compliment?'

Junior looks puzzled but doesn't answer.

'Of course I will. Shall we start at Liverpool Street so that we can change trains at Thorpe-le-Soken, like it says in the song?

Junior has a look of terror in his eyes. He grips my arm, even harder than last time and says with panic in his voice, 'No I can't do that yet. One step at a time please.'

'Okay then, let's go.'

'I'll drive us to the station,' declares Junior. He has hardly said the words before he flies out the door, races to the garage and starts his car up. He stops just long enough for me to get in and then drives with indecent haste down the driveway, scattering gravel in all directions, which is totally out of character.

'What's got into you? You NEVER drive like that, you are forever moaning about people who scuff your driveway. Now what is it?'

'I'm sorry. It's just that I have to do this. It's driving me nuts. I want to get back to normal. Do you know how scary it is to get lost on the underground and wake up at Liverpool Street station not knowing how you got there? I need to get my confidence back and I'm sure this will help.'

We arrive at the station, park the car, buy tickets and walk to the platform where the train is already waiting. Junior then has another panic attack.

'Are you sure this is the right train?'

'Oh for goodness sake! How did you manage last time on your own?'

'The train wasn't in then so I waited until it arrived. That way I knew which direction the train was going, this time it is in the platform and I didn't see it arrive so I don't know which way it is going.'

'Yes you do.'

'How?'

'Clue number one is the answer the ticket man gave you when you asked him the question. Clue number two is that when we walked past the driver's cab we could see the driver in place so we know which way he is going. He would hardly be likely to drive the train backwards now would he?'

'Fair point; I'll be alright when we get going.'

No sooner said than the train pulls away from the station. Junior breathes a huge sigh of relief. Twelve minutes and three stations later we are at Walton-on-the-Naze. We get off the train, leave the platform and are standing at the top of a hill looking over the town from our vantage point. I see the two towers that he has spoken about; the Martello Tower directly down the hill and across a field and then some way off in the distance on the far side of town stands the Naze Tower.

'Here we are Junior; this is it. Just how far did you get?'

'I walked towards that bend over there,' he says pointing in a direction 90° from the direction of the Martello Tower. Then I remember seeing the sea and a pier. At that point I panicked because if I had proceeded down that bit of a hill, gone round the corner and then looked back, I wouldn't have been able to see the station, so I didn't go any further. I retraced my steps, got back on the train and went home. What I want to do now is to walk a bit further and have you explain how you navigate.'

'This is ridiculous. You know perfectly well how to navigate.'

'Please! It's important to me. Getting lost on the underground has really spooked me.'

'So you said.'

'I need to build up my confidence again and I think if you talk me through your navigating method it might help me get back to normal.'

I pause before answering him, wondering if this is just an elaborate ruse but as this is the season of goodwill I decide to give him the benefit of the doubt even though the amber warning light is flashing in my head.

'Okay Junior, let's do it. We'll walk down the road that you started on and just keep going.'

'If you think it'll be alright.'

'It'll be alright,' I assure him. 'Just don't lose sight of me and you'll be fine.'

As we turn the corner and get out of sight of the railway station I can feel Junior tensing up.

'Relax will you, I know where I'm going.'

'You do?' he says rather uncertainly.

'I do; now when we get to the bottom of this short hill you will see the pier and the sea. When we get on the coast road we will head away from the pier but always keep the sea on our right hand side. Okay so far?'

'Yes, I think so.'

We carry on walking until we get to a fork in the road.

'Oh no!' sighs Junior.

'Now what's up?' I ask feeling rather irritated.

'Which road do we take? You know what you're like when you have a choice of two. You always pick the wrong one.'

'Not always; we'll take the right hand road.'

'So that means we go left.'

'No, it means we go right,' I insist. 'Now come on.'

We carry on walking until the road ends.

'There you are, I knew we should have gone left. The road ends here.'

'You are trying my patience Junior. Look beyond the road, you will see a footpath then another road and then in the distance you can see some grass and all the while the sea is on our right.'

'I'm sorry; I panicked. It doesn't take much these days. I'm still having nightmares about the underground.'

'So you keep saying.'

We carry on walking. The amber light is still flashing a warning in my head. Eventually we cover the distance that we could see from where Junior panicked and come to another choice of two possible routes, a road and a footpath behind some houses.

'Now what do we do?' he asks.

'You see the options; you choose.'

'Me? Why me?'

'Because you doubted my judgement last time so you choose this time and I'll follow without argument.'

He thinks for a moment and then decides. 'We'll take the footpath behind the houses because it's nearest to the sea and I remember what you said about keeping the sea on my right.'

I can sense Junior's confidence returning.

'Lead on.'

He does and I follow. In a couple of minutes he stops and stares at the Naze Tower.

'Wow, we've made it!' he says with an air of triumph.

'We have, and now if you look back when we get closer to the tower you will see the pier, so to get back to the station all you have to do is…..'

'I know; walk along the beach to the pier and then go straight up the road. Simple really isn't it!'

I don't answer but continue to walk towards the Naze Tower, which was built in 1720 by Trinity House as a navigation marker. In recent years it has been sold off, is now in private ownership and is home to an art gallery and a museum.

'Here we are Junior, we've made it,' I say pointing at the tower.

'Brilliant.'

'Did you know that in the summer you can climb up the inside and view the surrounding area from the top. It's an excellent view, you ought to do it sometime.'

'How do you know that?' he asks me.

'Because I've done it.'

'So you know this area then.'

'I do, very well as a matter of fact.'

He stares at me without answering but I can almost hear the cogwheels of his mind turning as he tries to work out if I am now stringing him along. We walk on past the tower more as a reflex action than anything else until we stop at the edge of a grass area that has been recently cut. Scanning the horizon I see the dockside cranes across the water.

'Do you know where those cranes are?' I ask Junior.

'No idea,' he answers.

'That is Felixstowe over there,' I say pointing.

'Felixstowe? That's miles away.'

'It is by road but not so far by water. Opposite Felixstowe but out of view is Harwich where the ferries sail from. Harwich has a lot of naval history attached to it and is well worth a look sometime. If you went there by train from the Walton station you would have to change trains twice, once at Thorpe and then again at Colchester.'

Junior looks panic stricken, 'Don't say that,' he begs.

'Say what?'

'Change trains; I can't do it once, never mind twice!'

'Drive then,' I say, 'and if you feel brave enough, park the car and catch the ferry to the Hook of Holland. If you can't bear to be parted from your car, drive that on to the ferry and drive off the other side at the Hook. Go and explore Europe. You are young, just do it instead of whingeing and whining about what might go wrong. The world is your oyster. Go and see it.'

Just as I finish telling him that my legs begin to wobble. The smile is wiped from my face in an instant.

'What was that Junior? My legs have turned to jelly. The ground is shaking. Are we having an earthquake?' It is my turn to panic. I try to hold my breath to calm myself down. My eyes are closed and just when I think, I'm back to normal, another violent shaking strikes at my legs. I open my eyes expecting to see the cranes at Felixstowe, but they've gone. The sky has gone. There is no sea. I start to panic again; then I see the whole space filled with Junior's face.

'Wake up,' he tells me firmly, shaking my leg.

'What?'

'Wake up,' he repeats.

I struggle to obey but eventually I realise that I'm not standing on the Naze near the tower looking across to Felixstowe, I'm sitting in an armchair.

'Come on, pull yourself together.'

'What happened? Where am I?' I ask but I know the answer before he tells me.

'You fell asleep after dinner and have been dreaming.'

'Dreaming? How do you know?'

'You mumbled a few things like "fairies". What was that all about?' he asks.

I am fully awake now and still have the dream in my head. I smile to myself when he says "fairies" when really it was "ferries". 'It doesn't matter Junior, you wouldn't believe me if I told you.'

'Try me,' he says.

'It was about navigation.'

'Navigation?' he queries. 'So if you aren't actually travelling around you dream about travelling do you?'

'Sometimes I do.'

'Where was it this time?'

'The dream has faded now; I can't remember the details exactly,' I say defensively.

'You're planning something aren't you? I know that look,' he says accusingly.

'You know me too well Junior. Let's just call it forward planning shall we?'

ND - #0138 - 080726 - C16 - 197/132/9 - PB - 9781780357980 - Gloss Lamination